Squalls and Rainbows

James K. Richardson

THE FLOATING YEARS / FLORIDA

SQUALLS AND RAINBOWS. Copyright © 2011 by James K. Richardson. All rights reserved. No part of this book may be reproduced or transmitted in any form or by any means, electronic or mechanical, including photocopying recording, or by any information storage and retrieval system, without written permission from James K. Richardson.

PRINTED IN THE UNITED STATES OF AMERICA

Visit our website at: www.TheFloatingYears.com

First edition published 2011.

ISBN-13: 978-0-9837181-0-9
ISBN-10: 0-9837181-0-5

For Karin

www.TheFloatingYears.com

Visit our web site for pictures and route charts of this cruise, and for information about our other cruises and books.

Cover photo of the Pitons on St. Lucia by the author.

Disclaimer

The latitude/longitude coordinates in this book and on our web site are approximate and for reference purposes only. They are not to be used for navigation.

ACKNOWLEDGMENTS

I first met Sam Mariani in high school when I dated his daughter. Sam introduced me to many new experiences, among them sailing. I crewed on his Ranger 27 and his Coronado 34 over several summers off the coast of New Jersey. Sam had a big heart, a first-rate intellect, and a passion for life that was infectious.

Murv Banner unofficially adopted me when he married my sister. Murv is a natural chef who understands that the ingredients are more important than the recipe; he is insightful, loving, and a wonderful story teller. He believed in me, and I owe a great deal to his example.

Many thanks to my brother Bob and sister-in-law Teresa for keeping us afloat during boatless years. From navigating thick fog near Atlantic City and stepping barefoot into a bucket of Barnegat Bay blue crabs, to cruising Charlotte Harbor, Florida, they generously shared their boating adventures.

I thank Ron Goldfarb, my lifelong friend, for sharing my love of the sea. We caught lobsters off New Jersey jetties, camped out in his Studebaker Lark to catch the tide at Montauk Point, Long Island, and explored coral reefs in the Florida Keys and Puerto Rico.

Karin and I are especially grateful for the friendship and assistance of the many cruisers and islanders we met along the way.

They changed our lives and made this book possible. Several are mentioned herein, but many are not. We are indebted to them all.

Thanks also to Hanni Schweer, for her extensive and detailed editing. Any leftover errors are my fault, not hers.

Finally, and most importantly, I thank my wife Karin. It was her interest in living aboard, and her willingness to leap from safe harbor, that made all our adventures possible. Once she got me to listen, we became an unbeatable team.

CONTENTS

INTRODUCTION 1

PART ONE OPERA AND GLOW WORMS

   LUPERON 8
   FRIENDS 15
   LUPERON HARBOR 20
   PUERTO PLATA 24
   WATERFALL SWIMMING 26
   ROAD OF SMILES 29
   CARNIVAL 35
   GLOWING GOODBYE 37

PART TWO DANCING WITH HURRICANES

   BRADENTON 43
   MARATHON 46
   CHUBB CAY 49
   GEORGETOWN 52
   GEORGETOWN TO THE TURKS AND CAICOS 57
   COCKBURN HARBOR 59
   SOUTH CAICOS TO THE DOMINICAN REPUBLIC 61

PART THREE WHALES AND PITONS

   BOQUERÓN 66
   SOUTHERN COAST OF PUERTO RICO 70
   BAHIA ICACOS 73
   CHARLOTTE AMALIE 77
   THE VIRGIN AND LEEWARD ISLANDS 79
   PRINCE RUPERT BAY 86
   LE MARIN 92
   RODNEY BAY 95

PART FOUR STEEL MUSIC AND SHARK BAKE

   RUNNING FROM EMILY 104
   CHAGUARAMAS 107

THE ENTREPRENEUR 111
THE MECHANIC 113
TURTLE BABIES 115
MUSICAL FOOD 118
MAYORA 122
PORT OF SPAIN 126
CENTRAL MARKET 128
THE POTTERY FACTORY AND TEMPLES 131
PITCH LAKE 134
RETURNING NORTH 136

PART FIVE NUTMEG BREEZE

PRICKLEY BAY 142
REVOLUTION, CHOCOLATE, AND RUM 145
A GIRL AND A BOY 149
CRUISE INTERRUPTED 151
WORKING BOAT RACES 155
TYRELL BAY 157
THE GRENADINES 160
RODNEY BAY 165
ST. LUCIA TO SINT MAARTEN 167
SIMPSON BAY LAGOON 171

PART SIX SQUALLS AND RAINBOWS

ENSENADA HONDA 180
CULEBRA TO SOUTH CAICOS 186
COCKBURN HARBOR 190
ABRAHAMS BAY 194
FISHERMAN'S BAY 198
CLARENCE TOWN 205
CONCEPTION ISLAND 210
THE RUN HOME 212
EPILOGUE 215

INTRODUCTION

We met in Chicago, far from any ocean to sail. Karin had grown up there. She had fond memories of the Gulf of Mexico from childhood vacations, but otherwise no connection to the sea. She did enjoy tent camping, however, and that was a start. I had relocated from New Jersey with salt water in my veins. I had frequented the Jersey beach and at thirteen had taken up SCUBA. My friend Ron and I carted our tanks to ocean inlets where we hunted lobsters lurking in the underwater rocks. We both developed an interest in oceanography and sailing. My then father-in-law owned a cruising sailboat. I was his crew for several years, and a weekend boatyard rat.

In 1988 Karin and I married. We had no plans involving water. Three years later we moved to Tampa on a job transfer. The next year, to celebrate Ron's fiftieth birthday, we chartered a sailboat out of St. Petersburg for an afternoon cruise. We brought Champagne and appetizers, and enjoyed a relaxing sail with a paid captain at the helm. There was a gentle breeze, the bay was flat, and at the Sunshine Skyway bridge we spotted dolphins.

"I really enjoyed that," Karin said afterward. "I think I could get into this sailing thing." Three months later we owned a 1976 Morgan 32 sloop, which we named *Cyana*.

We sailed *Cyana* on weekends and vacations. I was excited to own a boat and adventuresome to the point of recklessness. One afternoon I set full sail in a thirty knot blow to "see what the boat could handle." We crashed into six foot waves with the lee rail underwater. Karin was terrified. Suddenly the mainsail ripped, which sent her over the edge. She ran below and curled up in the forward bunk.

Karin did not give up, however. Instead, she worked at making me a better sailor. She encouraged me to think about what I was doing and to plan better. I became more prudent, focusing more on comfort and safety than thrills. I continued to push her too, to go places she never imagined. We soon ventured out of Tampa Bay and south along the Florida coast. Over time, we settled into roles that supported each other. We became a team.

We learned new skills. I became a diesel mechanic, a navigator, a plumber, an electrician, and a rigger. Karin took up canvas work and discovered a love of wood. She became expert at teak refinishing. She also learned the art of stocking up a boat for extended trips. We read books on the maritime trades, on sailing techniques, and cruising stories. We began to plan to move aboard and cruise.

We sold *Cyana* and bought a Pearson 365 ketch, which we named *Delphinium*. The extra four plus feet provided live-aboard space and the rig offered more sail plans. Unfortunately, for what we could afford, the boat was old, poorly equipped, and had suffered years of neglect. *Delphinium* became our college education in boat repair. She was my dream; she became Karin's nightmare. We both, however, honed our skills and gained valuable experience in boat work.

The day came when we put our house up for sale. We thought it would take six months, and by then *Delphinium* would be ready for us to move aboard. One week later we received an offer. The following day the company we both worked for closed their doors. We lost our income, our car, and our health insurance. We accepted the house offer. Before moving we held a large garage sale in which we sold most of our possessions.

Karin found a new job and we rented an apartment. We dedicated the next six months to bringing *Delphinium* back to life. For the first three months I worked every day in the boatyard with Karin helping on weekends. We then moved to a slip in St. Petersburg to continue the refurbishment.

We moved aboard in December of 1992 and lived the next fifteen years on *Delphinium* and her successor *Nalani*. Most of this time we held jobs while docked at various marinas from St. Petersburg to Sarasota. On weekends and vacations, when we weren't fixing or upgrading the boat, we sailed and anchored out.

In 1997 we quit our jobs and headed for the Bahamas. It was our first blue water cruising, our first crossing of the Gulf Stream, and our first taste of the islands. We had an inadequate alternator, no SSB radio, and no auxiliary power such as a wind generator. We didn't have an oven nor use refrigeration. It was bare bones cruising. We sailed down the Exuma Islands to Georgetown.

This first cruise convinced us of two things: (1) we wanted to do it again, and (2) we needed a better boat. We sold *Delphinium* and bought a Tayana 37, which we named *Nalani*.

It took five years to build up our funds and to upgrade *Nalani*. Unlike *Delphinium*, she was in good condition, but her former owners only day-sailed; she had no cruising equipment. The day finally came in 2003 when we quit our jobs again, to sail away a second time. We retraced our route to the Exuma Islands and then ventured farther to Cat Island and Long Island. *Nalani* was stronger, safer, and more comfortable. She had a powerful alternator and refrigeration, and we had added a sailing vane to help steer. There were new electronics and many other improvements. We wrote about our two cruises to the Bahamas in *White Cays and Blue Seas*.

We were ready to go beyond the Bahamas. This is the story of our next cruise, through the Bahamas and the Turks and Caicos to the

Caribbean Sea. From the Dominican Republic to Puerto Rico, through the Virgin islands, and south along the Eastern Caribbean islands to Trinidad, South America.

Visit **www.TheFloatingYears.com** for pictures and route charts.

Part One

Opera and Glow Worms

Nalani sways side to side as her bow lifts to the star-speckled sky and then genuflects to the black sea. Wires rattle against the mast, playing strings to the bass percussion of the diesel engine. The sails are loosely tied on deck. The boat had creaked and clattered and rolled all night, without any wind in the sails to steady her. Sleep had been impossible. We had last seen land at lunch the day before, anchored off Sand Cay on the Caicos Banks.

Dawn slowly dissolves the black night, unveiling a puffy, gray sky. The air is crisp and clean, with a tang of moist salt. The sea is churned by high swells with deep valleys, stretching out to the horizon. A slight breeze forms and ripples the surface. The sun gains strength and begins to burn off the mist ahead. Suddenly mountains emerge, like distant ships from the fog. Great gray titans of jagged rock, splashed in sunlight, rise high into billowing white clouds. It is a triumphant pallet of grays and yellows, painted on a canvas of white mist and blue sky.

We stare awe-struck. Hispaniola lies ahead. The realization sweeps over us in a moment of clarity. Flush with anticipation, our anxious spirits soar.

LUPERON
DOMINICAN REPUBLIC
19° 58' N   70° 57' W

We followed the red dinghy into Luperon Harbor. At the helm was one of the permanent liveaboards. He had come out that morning to guide the new arrivals past the shoals. We found an open spot, dropped our anchor, and shut down the engine.

Nalani floated wonderfully quiet in the calm harbor. We were exhausted, but excited. It was three months to the day since we had left Bradenton, Florida. The last 24 hours we had been at sea with no sleep. Our tired smiles barely concealed our glee; we had made our first truly foreign landfall. We hauled up the yellow Q flag, declaring quarantine, and waited for El Commandante.

El Commandante was variously portrayed as a even-tempered gentleman, as a rule-happy autocrat, or as a military dictator. We had no idea of what to expect, and having little confidence in our sparse Spanish, we waited with some trepidation.

A small boat approached. A fellow cruiser was at the helm; his expression showed a thin smile of relief. Seated with him were three Dominicans. The one propped up in front, his head noticeably above the others, was clearly El Commandante. He was wearing pressed green fatigues, a U.S. Navy hat, and a white shirt adorned with epaulets. His elegant Spanish nose was lifted high, as if sniffing improprieties. A lanky young assistant slumped lazily behind him. The third Dominican sat properly bored. The boat's engine whined, as they sloshed through the brown water.

"Permission to board," the tall, lanky one said, as the boat nudged against our hull. The three did not wait for an answer. They scrambled over our life lines, ignoring the open gate.

"Yes, of course," I responded lamely, as they tramped across our deck in black boots, leaving smudge marks. They plopped onto the seats in our cockpit. Up close, El Commandante was surprisingly small; at a distance, his officious demeanor and posture had made him appear larger. He sat stiffly upright and stared uninterested across the harbor. The tall one introduced himself as Benjamin and pulled out a pile of forms. El Commandante meticulously examined his fingernails.

After filling out several forms, Benjamin asked to go below. He glanced around the cabin, making a show of opening cabinets and peering into drawers. As he moved about he recited a memorized speech about how much the Navy does to protect their foreign visitors, how they patrol the coast and harbor, and how they assist vessels in distress. The waters were only safe due to their hard work and diligence.

"Of course, " he added, "you might want to make a completely voluntary donation." He did not say the donation would actually go to the Navy. I smiled and offered nothing. He droned on some more and then asked again. I smiled. After a third try, he shrugged and climbed back up to the cockpit, mumbling something in Spanish. El Commandante quickly turned sour. He made a show of his displeasure by pressing a nostril and blowing his nose on our deck. I worried that the visit might turn unfriendly.

Karin defused the tension by handing out chocolate muffins she had baked. Benjamin's eyes grew wide and he smiled broadly. He wolfed his down in a few large bites. A thin smile broke El Commandante's stoic expression. He nibbled an edge and launched into rapid animated Spanish, incomprehensible to us, but clearly in praise of the fine merits of the muffin, and then he caught himself and stiffened. He carefully wrapped the muffin in its napkin and set it on his lap.

Benjamin asked us to ferry them to the next boat. I explained that our dinghy was tied down and it would require some time to set up, and anyway it was really too small. Certainly they would be more comfortable calling for their boat. Well, it turned out the Navy had no boat. Perturbed, but accepting the inevitable, I untied and launched our dinghy. I decided, however, not to install the engine. We would row, as my protest.

The four of us climbed into our three-person dinghy and pushed off. We waddled slowly forward, rowing against the tide precariously low on our lines. El Commandante posed in the bow, his back stiff and his nose up, surveying his kingdom, while carefully cradling his chocolate muffin. Benjamin nervously scanned the harbor, looking for help. After a few minutes, he spotted another cruiser in an inflatable with an outboard and waved frantically. This was how I met Emil.

Emil later told us how he had watched with great amusement as the overloaded dinghy tipped and swayed in the current. The self-important officials had lost all control, and they looked as if they feared for their lives. He had decided to help, and was on his way, when Benjamin spotted him. Emil towed us to the next boat.

Later that morning, after attaching the outboard, we motored through the maze of anchored yachts to town. We tied up at the muelle, a long cement pier that leads into the village of Luperon. It was crowded with small boats: cruiser dinghies, shiny new and weathered old, and local skiffs, sun-faded, muddy, and chipped. There were two abandoned rowboats tied by frayed lines and half underwater, barnacle encrusted and rotted. We scrambled onto the pier for our first solid footing in days.

We passed a young couple on a romantic stroll who smiled brightly when we said "hola." Two children were climbing the rocks at water's edge, looking for whatever children look for. They noticed us and scrambled up to follow. They held out their hands, palms up, and repeated "peso, peso." We ignored them and they soon gave up. We passed a circle of young men, laughing and drinking bottles of El Presidente, the local beer. They politely ignored us until we smiled and said "hola." They smiled broadly then, and nodded, returning our greeting. We marveled at how handsome Dominicans are, a mixture of Spanish and Indian, with oriental traces.

Tied to the muelle was an old motor yacht, outfitted with guns and flying the Dominican flag. It was adorned with navy signs. A sailor was fishing off the bow. At the end of the muelle, we came upon a soldier propping a sub-machine gun on his hip. He nodded unsmiling as we passed. We scurried into the long trailer labeled "Inmigración."

Inside there was a reception desk with offices on either side. We were greeted by a clerk whose English was about as good as our Spanish. He scribbled something on a form and then led us to the first office. A tall, elegant man, with the sculpted features of an aristocrat, stood and greeted us with a wide smile and handshake.

"I am the chief," he announced in impeccable English. He motioned for us to sit and closed the door.

The chief welcomed us to Luperon and asked about our travels. He was disarmingly friendly and relaxed, as if he was personally curious about us. He was clearly sizing us up, though, deciding if we warranted a more thorough examination. We apparently passed, as he shook our hands again and turned us over to the clerk next door. This began a process of filling out forms and handing over money, to one clerk after another, each in a different office. They were friendly and efficient, speaking just enough English to guide us through their particular form. They all understood U.S. dollars quite well.

The sun was hot when we emerged from Inmigración, our clearance papers in hand. The stack of officiously stamped forms had cost us $78 U.S. We were elated; our boat was legal, we were legal, and our use of the harbor was approved. We had even been deemed agriculturally acceptable. Although we never experienced any real difficulties clearing in or out of a country, we always felt a great sense of relief when it was done.

We studied our map of Luperon. The muelle access road forks into two main streets which run through the village and join again at a highway that leads into the country. These main streets are intersected by numerous cross streets crowded with shops, bars, restaurants, and small homes. The homes are one story with two or three rooms. They are sided with wood slats and painted in faded blues, yellows, greens, and whites. They are topped with rust encrusted corrugated steel. Ventilation is provided by generous gaps in the siding, by broken and rotted slats, and by open doors and windows. Many have wooden chairs set outside the front door, to chat with passersby.

The streets were busy with cars and motor bikes, and the sidewalks were crowded. Pickup trucks sold fruits and vegetables piled high in their beds: bananas, mangos, eggplants, cabbages, assorted roots, oranges and more. Music, horns, shouts, and engine noise filled the air. Drainage gullies ran along the edges of the streets collecting dirty water, fruit peels, egg shells, and other garbage, including the occasional dead rat. This effluent makes its way slowly to the harbor where it mixes with fuel spills, bilge discharge, and boat toilets, eventually settling to the bottom in a thick, gray muck. You don't want to swim in the harbor.

We walked into town and found the Verizon office (formerly Code-a-Tel), which provided the twin necessities of currency exchange and internet access. Pesos were 29 to the dollar, and internet was a meager 10 pesos (about 30 cents) for ten minutes. We viewed our accumulated email messages, and sent out an arrival notice to friends and family.

With fresh pesos in our pockets, we crossed the street and climbed the wide stairs into "Steve's." Steve is an American expatriate who married a local Dominican and settled to raise a family. He and his wife run a restaurant and bar, pool hall, laundry, and motor bike rental. He built the building himself. It's one elevated floor with a strong cement structure and a thatch roof with open sides. Steve and his wife are friendly and helpful, speak fluent English, and offer exotic treats like smoked pork chops and American-style breakfasts. They have the cleanest rest room in town, with signs instructing users not to flush toilet paper, to use the waste can instead. The town sewer system is fragile. The electrical source is also unreliable, which explained the candles. Steve's is a kind of halfway house between cruiser and local cultures. It's a good place to begin the transition, and to sip your first El Presidente.

We quizzed Steve about the town and his life in Luperon, while we enjoyed that beer. We then ventured out for lunch. We chose Laisas, a small luncheonette favored by locals. There were only a half-dozen tables, but they did a good take-out business. We picked two empty chairs and ordered the daily special. It was fried chicken with rice and peas and a salad. It was delicious and the portions were generous, at a bargain $4.00 U.S. per person. We were the only foreigners in the place, but we were politely served and nicely ignored, except by the flies and the dogs that beg under the tables.

After lunch we walked up the street. Siesta was underway. Formerly open doors and windows were shuttered closed. It was just as well; our excitement had mellowed, and a good siesta was an appealing thought.

We were dazed by the new sights and experiences, flush in the emotions of our landfall. We glowed with pride at what we had accomplished: the preparation and planning, the skills developed, and the hard work. Our hearts brimmed with the excitement of new adventures to come. But most of all we were immensely relieved. We were safe in a calm and secure harbor and cleared through customs. The nervous uncertainty of the sea voyage was over.

As we approached *Nalani* she looked different somehow, settled and smug, at home.

FRIENDS

One of the joys of cruising is the people you meet. Some are fellow cruisers and some are island locals, but they are all memorable. Each of these hearty and adventurous types has their own interesting story. Occasionally, you develop a true friendship. There were three special couples we met on this cruise.

Charly and Francoise cruised aboard *Bobato*, a 55-foot fast trawler, or slow motor yacht, if you prefer. With only one cabin down forward with the galley and heads, *Bobato* had a large salon and a roomy afterdeck. While most motor yacht captains preferred swanky marinas, *Bobato* could usually be found swinging at anchor among the sailboats, mast-less, as if suffering an identity crisis. She was like the wolf raised by sheep who thought of herself as a bald sheep. Charly and Francoise were true cruisers and they were more comfortable among other cruisers.

Charly had decided in his early thirties to try sailing. He found a boat, negotiated a price, and then asked the owner to teach him to sail. After a few lessons he packed his clothes, moved aboard, and set sail -- for Brazil, from France. Along the way he figured out how to use a sextant, which was a good plan since he found Brazil. That was

30 years ago, and except for the recent move to *Bobato* Charly had lived on one sailboat after another, cruising around the world.

He was anchored off Martinique in a Jeanneau 47 sailboat when he met Francoise. She ran a crepe business, supplying local restaurants. Francoise was not afraid of hard work, nor afraid of risk. She hopped aboard and they sailed across the Pacific, visiting South Seas islands on the way to Australia. There they sold the sailboat and flew to New York, where they bought *Bobato*.

After a major refit they headed to the Bahamas where we met them in the restaurant at Chubb Cay Marina in the Berry Islands. We had arrived that same day, after crossing the Gulf Stream from Marathon, Florida. It was our tradition after the all-night arduous crossing to celebrate with a delicious meal of fried conch and Nassau grouper, drink plenty of wine, and have a sound sleep docked in the flat calm of the marina.

Charly and Francoise were wonderfully warm and outgoing, and we exchanged histories. It was friendship at first sight. We crossed paths many times on our cruise and ultimately developed a lasting relationship.

I first met Emil when he tossed a line from his motor-powered dinghy rescuing me from rowing El Commandante against the current. A year later Emil remembered the incident fondly. But then Emil and his wife Olena view everything in life fondly. They are rare people, the kind that see only good in the world, and if anything bad happens to them, they find a way to turn it upside down into something good.

We had heard them on the radio, crossing at night from the Turks and Caicos to Luperon. In their Morgan Out-Island 41, *Unicorn*, they were one of a half-dozen sailboats who made the crossing together. We got to know them in Luperon, and like Charly and Francoise we crossed paths regularly down island. They too became good friends.

Emil was born in the Ukraine and emigrated to Canada with his parents during World War II. He grew up, married, had children, and worked for the government. The marriage didn't last, but as he was nearing retirement he met Olena in the Ukraine, on a government project. She joined him in Canada and they married. Emil retired, Olena took a sabbatical, and they bought a boat to go cruising. They were fearless and determined, but novices in boating. They were fast learners, though, with good judgment and sharp instincts, the kind of people who face any problem down until it begs to be let go. They could accomplish anything they set out to do.

Emil has a sharp mind and is well-versed in politics. He refuses to preach his opinions though, preferring to listen. You always think you have convinced him he is so eager to hear, and is so respectful of, your viewpoint. If he disagrees, he simply raises a minor counter point, as if he had heard someone else espouse it, but then he quickly agrees you are probably right. He is not muddled in his thinking – far from it; he is simply polite to a fault. This makes you listen more attentively to him to discern his real opinion. He is political in a truly positive manner.

Olena is also very intelligent and independent minded. She worked as a consultant for the Canadian government, developing health care in third world countries. She was never far from email between assignments. These two seemed supremely out of place on a cruising boat until you got to know them. Then, you understood it was simply another challenge for them to overcome.

Divya is tall and beautiful, with a quiet self-assuredness and an understated intelligence. She was once a professional opera singer, but she does not behave the part. Chris is a large amiable bear of a man, with a thin beard and a somewhat disheveled look, like his clothes are never arranged right. His innocent curiosity and gentle politeness allow him to breach any etiquette without consequences.

On Friday nights cruisers and locals gather at Puerto Blanco Marina, to enjoy the weekly buffet and a night out. The marina is tucked into the mangroves on the northwest side of the harbor, a few hundred yards from the competitive Marina Luperon. The restaurant and bar is roofed with open sides and has a Karaoke stand near the entrance.

One Friday Divya took the Karaoke microphone and waited patiently for her song. She was ignored; a din of loud conversations, glasses clinking, plates scraping, and laughter rose like smoke from the crowd. The deceptively timid *Over the Rainbow* started and nobody noticed. Divya began to sing, softly at first, as if not wanting to interrupt. Quiet spread like fire as people looked up from their food and turned away from conversations. Beer bottles and forks settled on tables. Divya raised her voice and attacked the notes with an incredible emotional inflection. Applause erupted spontaneously. Everyone was shocked, as much by the performance as by hearing it in a bar in Luperon.

Her husband Chris then ambled up to the microphone and now nobody knew what to expect. He called up four other cruisers to stand beside him and launched into a spirited version of *But will you still love me tomorrow*. As he sang, the cruisers danced and twirled, and like a backup band filled in on the chorus. It was hilarious, and as entertaining as Divya was artistic. Chris added a new verse which he had scratched out on a bar napkin. It spoke of cruisers following the directions of Bruce Van Sant, author of the popular and commonly used *Gentleman's Guide to Passages South*. Van Sant lived part-time in Luperon and was in the audience that night.

Chris and Divya sailed out of New England on the *Maggie M* each year to winter south. They usually stay in the Bahamas, but this year they made it to Luperon. The *Maggie M* is an older, traditional sailing ship, with the many quirks and worn out equipment that come with such a vessel. Chris and Divya learned that things break and plans go awry, and they learned about navigation and weather. Like true cruisers, they never let the problems dampen their enthusiasm. They have the ability to shed difficulties like so many learning experiences, continuing on, filled with good spirit.

LUPERON HARBOR

The muddy harbor, and the village of Luperon, are surrounded by hills, as if cupped in large hands. The hills protect Luperon from the storms of nature and people, but they also isolate it. The vast country beckoning from the road out of town, and the wild ocean a short hike away, fade from your awareness. You are quickly assimilated into the busy charm of the village, and the bustling community of the harbor. The calm, consistent weather, rarely too hot and never chilly, lulls you into a relaxed contentment.

The harbor is filled with anchored boats; a few leave each day and more arrive to take their place. Some of these are simply cruising by; they lay over a few days for supplies and rest. Some, like us, stay weeks, or even months, to learn something of the country and its people. Then there are those who set a permanent anchor, adopting Luperon as their home. The harbor is truly a community with its own rhythms; it has a hierarchy of important people and implicit rules of behavior. It wakes with the sun and settles with the last beer at night. Evenings are quiet, with dinghies crisscrossing the harbor to visit friends on other boats, to dine or drink in town, or to party at a marina. Everyone is considerate, and aware of how sound travels over the water.

Most days we woke with the sun, as the parade of local fisherman passed by on their way to sea. Their voices shouted over the loud popping of their outboards and their wakes slapped our hull. They were marking their territory, waking the gringos to a new dawn. We usually ate a simple breakfast of coffee, fruit, and yogurt. We brewed yogurt each day in glass jars from a carton of long-life milk, heated gently with leftover yogurt as Francoise had taught us. Some days we ate a hearty breakfast of eggs, ham, and potatoes, and skipped lunch.

There was plenty to do. After breakfast, we loaded the dinghy and headed into town, or over to the Puerto Blanco marina. We had to discard garbage, do laundry, refill jugs of water, and top up our diesel, gasoline, and propane. Every couple of days we ran the engine to charge the house battery bank, and this necessitated regular oil and filter changes, and other minor engine service. The teak deck and rails needed cleaning and polishing. Every few weeks the anchor had to be hauled up and cleaned of mud; if not, it sunk ever deeper and eventually would be permanently gone. The boat bottom needed regular scraping of barnacles, coral, and algae. For this task, one look over the side was enough to convince us to pay another boater who ran a small business cleaning boat bottoms. There were emails to check, shopping to do, books to read, and naps to take. This was living afloat.

There were three small grocery stores and two bakeries in town, each often sold out of most products. We would pick up a few fruits or vegetables, and maybe some meat, at each one. When we were desperate, or in want of a treat, we would raid Steve's freezer for smoked pork chops. Sometimes we would be lucky to be in town when one of the farmer pickup trucks parked on the street, its bed filled with eggplants, peppers, limes, pineapples, and other produce. The grocery stores, locals, and cruisers shared this occasional bounty. Fish was quickly sold to restaurants and stores, but sometimes overflow was available at the front steps of a fisherman's house.

We usually ate lunch in town or at one of the marinas. Steve's had good sandwiches and daily specials prepared by his Dominican wife. Letty's offered delicious Creole chicken and fish. Gina's served a huge hamburger ala American. Puerto Blanco was always good for simple local food. Marina Luperon had a great view of the harbor and an upscale European menu. Lunches out were barely more expensive than buying and preparing the food ourselves. It was also an opportunity to learn more about the people and their foods. We reserved our cooking for dinners when we preferred to stay aboard.

Puerto Blanco Marina was the place to be in the early evenings. The clientele were an eclectic mix of cruisers and locals, and the beer and food were cheap. This was the office for the permanent liveaboards, where matters of importance to the community were discussed and decisions made. These regulars were joined by the temporarily anchored, by local residents, and by ex-pat Americans who had relocated to houses in the hills. Social demarcations melted over cold El Presidentes; we learned about each other's lives, problems, and achievements. Some nights the crowd overflowed the roofed bar to the outside decks. Dinner was always available, and on Friday nights the buffet and music drew especially large crowds, including a few older aristocrats with teenage girlfriends on their arms.

One night there was to be a "sing along" with professional jazz singers and a highly touted banjo player, the author of popular cruising guides. The usual good food and cheap beer contributed to the draw.

At 7 p.m. we sat at a table with Charly, Francoise, Emil, and Olena, finishing up our dinner. Chris was at the bar drinking El Presidentes, a guitar slung over his shoulder. The advertised entertainment were nowhere to be seen. We ordered another round of beers and waited. We ordered more beers and waited some more. This was not a serious imposition, as we enjoyed the company and the night out. Finally, prodded by several people who took note of his guitar, Chris spun around on his stool and announced he would sing a few songs that he had written.

Chris played remarkably well, and his songs were unique and interesting. One tune in particular, a song he wrote about the bayous of Louisiana, brought down the house. The theme was "dangly things hanging all around," and it was very amusing. After midnight, we wove our dinghy through the harbor back to *Nalani* on a considerably less than straight path.

This was our busy daily life. Occasionally we found time to hike up the surrounding hills to wander among the local farms, or to cross to the ocean for a walk on the beach. We took a few dinghy excursions out of the harbor to nearby bays to watch fish jump and see the local birds and flowers. And, of course, we scheduled visits inland to see the country.

PUERTO PLATA

Our first trip outside Luperon was to Puerto Plata. Emil and Olena picked us up early one morning in their inflatable. After tying up at the muelle, we walked through Luperon to where the main roads rejoin at the highway out of town. There we found a Gua-Gua, a small car which runs back and forth to Imbert where you can catch a bus to Puerto Plata. Karin sat on my lap up-front, while Emil and Olena got stuffed rather intimately into the back with two other passengers. It cost us one dollar U.S. for a 30 minute trip, so you get the idea. At Imbert, instead of waiting for the next bus, we pooled our fares and hired a car.

We drove through rolling hills lush with tropical trees and bushes and by roadside stands overflowing with bananas. We passed motorcyclists carting huge propane cylinders and farmers riding donkeys with long machetes hanging off their belts. Along the roadside were cement houses and tin shacks and fields of green sugar cane shimmering in the breeze. In the distance, misty mountains rose into blue sky. The pace was frantic with cars and motorcycles running corners recklessly and jockeying to pass each other.

The driver dropped us at Parque Central in Puerto Plata where we were cornered by a young man intent on directing us around town.

We tried several times to shake him but he refused to leave. We figured he was paid a commission by the tourist shops he pushed us towards. Finally, easy going Emil had had enough; he shouted angrily: "No Assisto." The guide shrugged and walked away.

We found the Tanio Art Museum on the second floor of a shopping building. The Tanio were pre-Columbian Indians who populated Hispaniola before being decimated by small pox and the Spanish. Their ancient pottery and figurines were displayed in glass cabinets. Next we found the Amber Museum. Amber is crystallized resin and common in Hispaniola. On display were rare jewels embedded with flowers, insects, and even reptile fossils. On our walk we also stopped at several stores selling Larimar, a semi-precious stone found only in the Dominican Republic.

We descended the hilly streets to the waterfront and the Fuerte de San Felipe, for which the town is famous. It is reported to be the first fort built by the Spanish in the new world, in 1540. The fort was a nicely refurbished network of small rooms and cannons. We then strolled the malecon, the walkway along the sea. East of town the coast was quite scenic with fat rolling waves crashing over large rock formations. We enjoyed a lunch of chicken and fish with rice, and several cold El Presidentes.

After lunch, we walked to the Super Mercado Tropical where we stuffed groceries, wine, and rum into our back packs. Exhausted, we hailed a taxi to return to Parque Central to find a bus back home. Unfortunately, we discovered that the buses did not leave from Parque Central. Instead, we had another long trek to La Rotunda where we found a bus to Imbert, and from there a taxi to Luperon.

That night we feasted on the rare treats we found in Puerto Plata: fresh bread, Sosua cheese, ham, and salami.

WATERFALL SWIMMING

In the hills near Imbert there is an amazing waterfall. Actually, there are twenty some waterfalls stacked one above the other, fed by a common stream. Each level is surrounded by rock, forming a grotto with a pool fed by a chute from the room above. Its pool overflows into a chute to the room below. It's a popular attraction, a Dominican theme park.

Early one morning, we, Chris and Divya, and two other cruising couples, loaded into Jose's van. Jose is handsome and well spoken, with a contagious smile and an honest desire to please. He is popular and makes a good living taking cruisers on various tours. We were in good spirits and excited.

At the parking area near the falls Jose pulled over to hire a local guide. The guide was a specialist, we learned, and Jose was pleased to share some of his income for the assistance. Gabrielle was tall, handsome, and well-muscled. He promptly led us to a path across a field, past grazing cattle with mountains in the background. The path wound through a forest and crossed a rocky stream several times. The trees formed canopies over colorful bushes and flowers.

We emerged from the woods at a pool, which was the lowest level of the falls. A rushing river of water cascaded down a chute from the rock above. The tumbling water was cool and tinted brown with tannin; it filled the air with mist. This was a place you could sit for hours and contemplate life, except that the previous tour was finishing, and the next tour would soon replace you. We enjoyed the experience for our allotted few minutes.

Gabrielle then climbed up the chute and braced himself against the rushing water. Jose followed, staying lower. One at a time, Jose pulled each of us up the chute and handed us to Gabrielle, who pulled us the rest of the way to next level. It looked easy, but when it was my turn I stumbled, finding it hard to get a foothold against the power of rushing water. Jose pulled and I pushed and eventually Gabrielle yanked me up the steepest part, where I was mostly underwater. I now understood his muscles.

The next level had its own pool, its own chute of cascading water, and its own cavern walls. From this private grotto, you could not see the level above. We collapsed around the pool and rested. Then, we repeated the process to get to the next level. In this manner, we climbed up six levels. Our guides explained there were many more levels, but we would stop there. As we rested by the pool, Jose explained how to get back down.

"Sit at the top of the chute. Drop your head to your chest, tuck in your arms, and keep your legs together," he instructed. It sounded easy.

I took my turn, reminding myself to stay tucked. I felt a slight push and off I went, flying down the chute carried by the rushing water. My arms and legs flailed uncontrolled as I slid over the water-smoothed rock. At the final turn I soared out the chute like a shot cannonball and crashed into the pool. I sank and kept sinking, unable to stop. It was frightening having no control over my descent. I then stalled and was able to stroke upwards to catch a breath.

I swam to the side of the pool and climbed out. I couldn't wait for the next chute. This was a water ride that would make Disney proud, and it was all natural. Karin came flying down and swam over smiling.

"Can I jump off the cliff," Chris asked, gazing over the side to the pool below.

"Sure," said Gabrielle, "Just aim for the deep water."

Chris jumped. I opted out, deciding to let him be the pioneer. I flew down the chute again. At the next level I saw that Chris was still breathing, so I gathered my courage. I studied the water, looking for the deepest part, and marveled at the height. I hesitated. They wouldn't let me do this if it wasn't safe, would they? Then I remembered where I was, and I realized that I alone was responsible for my safety. Oh well. I jumped.

The air rushed past as I dropped like a boulder. When I hit the water I kept dropping. Luckily the pool was indeed deep. After that, I alternated jumps and chutes the rest of the way down.

At the bottom pool I sat on the edge and waited for the rest of our party. When I looked up I was shocked to see Karin holding Jose's hand at the edge of the cliff. Karin is deathly afraid of heights. When we first met she couldn't even walk up a hill without becoming violently upset. She couldn't stand on a ladder. That she would even consider jumping off a cliff was astounding, and totally unbelievable.

I held my breath, fully expecting her to shake it off and step back. Instead, in one motion she let go of Jose's hand and leapt off the cliff. I was truly amazed, and incredibly proud of her.

ROAD OF SMILES

(first published in the Caribbean Compass Magazine www.caribbeancompass.com)

It erupts in an instant, that Dominican smile, overwhelming a practiced aloofness with an explosion of recognition, fondness, and genuine pleasure. It is something to behold, a flash of dazzling sunlight that warms your heart.

We rented a four-wheel drive Suzuki with Chris and Divya and headed out for the mountains. We followed the usual route from Luperon through Imbert to Puerto Plata, and from there we headed inland to Santiago. There were gorgeous views around most corners, the first looking back across farmed fields to the Atlantic ocean. We climbed up and down hills, more up than down, until we crossed the top of the mountain.

We descended the other side slowly, watching the valley of Santiago come into view. The valley emerges as a metropolis of buildings and roads, spread like some huge lake over the flatlands. Santiago is a large city with supermarkets, hardware stores, pharmacies, restaurants – anything you might need. We had decided to save our shopping for the return trip, but we treated ourselves to lunch at Pez Dorado on Calle Del Sol. We had rainbow trout in garlic sauce, and two of their pastas. The service and ambiance were top notch; the food was delicious.

After lunch we took the Autopista south. This is a serious four-lane highway. We found the turnoff to Jarabacoa around 20 kilometers later. There, a mostly paved road leads up into the central mountains. Jarabacoa is a resort town near three waterfalls and is famous for its art galleries. We drove through the town to the hotel Pinar Dorado. The parking lot was empty, except for a wandering herd of cattle.

Pinar Dorado looks like a 1960's Howard Johnson, but is finished inside with dramatic rock and wood walls decorated with art. There is a pool and an outdoor bar, a large restaurant, and the rooms are air-conditioned with hot water. This was luxury to boat people. For dinner we enjoyed beef fillets and pasta, with a bottle of red wine. As the only guests we were pampered, even though no English was spoken. From here on we had to pool our Spanish and point a lot to make ourselves understood.

The next day we drove to Salto Baiguate, one of the three nearby waterfalls. A few kilometers from the hotel we found the barely passable dirt road that leads through a small village and farm fields to the parking area of the falls. On the way we stopped to ask a farmer and his wife about their crops. They graciously gave us a half-dozen chayotes, green pear-shaped squash that they grew on trellises.

At the falls parking area we were approached by a young boy, probably the farmer's son. He was maybe seven or eight years old. He assured us with a determined, serious expression, that he would protect our "concho." He and his dog sat down next to the Suzuki, and he studied his wrist watch.

The path to the falls ran along the top of a cement water conduit. At the end we descended a set of wide stairs to the pool at the bottom of the falls. Water cascaded off a 100 foot cliff. Clouds of mist wafted through the air. The pool fed a rocky stream which wound off into the distance. Cliffs rose around us on three sides. Flowers adorned the bushes and grasses.

When we returned to our SUV our guard was on-duty, checking his watch with a very determined expression. He took his job quite seriously. He stood and started to walk away without asking for any money. It was simply his duty to protect the innocent Americanos. We handed him a few pesos and he smiled for the first time, a beautiful Dominican smile.

The packed-dirt road from Jarabacoa quickly narrows as it weaves up into the mountains on the way to Constanza. To one side a sheer drop tumbles off the mountain; to the other side a drainage ditch that could break an axle hugs the road, and beyond the ditch a cliff rises straight up. There are no guard rails and no curbs, but there are plenty of pot-holes, ruts, and bumps. There is hardly room for two cars to pass, and yet delivery trucks and motorcycles whiz by fearlessly. Donkeys and horses meander aimlessly. The rushes of adrenaline are fast and furious.

As we drove up this difficult dirt road we passed by steep cliffs of sheer rock, rolling hills lush with trees, bushes, and flowers, and terraced farms of layered rows of produce. The valleys were painted in dazzling greens and soft browns. There were donkeys, cows, and Brahma bulls; there were coffee bushes speckled with green and red beans; there were fields of squash, potatoes and other produce. And there was always a looming mountain range in the distance to frame the sky.

We careened around curves at five miles per hour, fearful of falling off. As we passed through each village one of us would hang out a window and point ahead, shouting to an amused villager: "Constanza?." The answer was always "si" with a nod, followed by sign language that clearly meant "it's a long, long, way, and very snake-like."

We focused on keeping our wheels on the road and avoiding the holes, trucks, motorcycles, and donkeys. Between gasps of fear we marveled at the scenery.

As we passed through villages we saw school children in uniforms, happily walking up the road. There were adults gathered at stores and in groups alongside the road. Their facial features changed with the altitude, increasingly favoring Indian ancestors. They hailed us with "hello" or "hola," and shouted "adios" as we passed, their faces exploding in that truly contagious Dominican smile.

Three hours later we reached El Rio and joined a paved road that led up more mountains. We passed roadside stands selling strawberry jam, and young men carrying trays of strawberries to cars. Around one final turn the valley of Constanza opened up before our eyes.

The valley is a huge bowl, reportedly created by a meteor. The soil is black and fertile with farms of every description spread across the flat land. They grow broccoli, cauliflower, potatoes, chayotes, fruits, flowers, eggplant, carrots, and much more. The village lies in the center of the valley. The view from atop that mountain is something we will never forget.

We descended the mountain and drove through the fields to the village of Constanza, where we stopped for lunch at Lorenzo's. After lunch we began a hunt for hotel space. Alto Cerro looked promising, up on a hill overlooking the valley and town, but they said they were filled. This was hard to believe as it was clearly off-season. Probably, they meant closed.

Ranchero Montana was closed for the season. Hotel San Remo was in the middle of town and had no air-conditioning, or even screens on the windows. We then found Mi Cabana where we rented a two apartment villa, upstairs and downstairs. The upstairs had a great view of the valley and mountains, and we flipped a coin for it. The winners invited the losers upstairs for rum cocktails, as a consolation.

After cocktails we drove into town and found the Aguas Blanca restaurant empty but open. We feasted on Pollo Cordon Blue and beef fillets, one with a brown mushroom and onion sauce, the other with a tomato, onion, and garlic sauce. This was washed down with two excellent red wines from their extensive collection. We tasted their soups, which were truly outstanding, and had fresh strawberries for dessert.

We eased back to the hotel to discover two other guests had checked in. We were no longer alone.

The next morning we awoke to roosters and then returned to Lorenzos for a breakfast of fried eggs, sautéed potatoes, fried green plantains, and coffee. After breakfast, while the rest of us shopped, Chris returned to the hotel to retrieve his false tooth. He had inadvertently left it behind. Chris spoke no Spanish so Divya made him memorize the word for "tooth," which he promptly forgot. When he arrived at the hotel, he simply pointed at the gap in his teeth. The desk clerk flashed another of those famous Dominican smiles and handed him the tooth, delicately wrapped in a napkin.

We left Constanza and returned to El Rio, continuing east on Route 12 instead of north to Jarabacoa over the dirt mountain road. Route 12 is paved and actually has guard rails for most of its winding trek through the mountains. We made better time and had a much easier drive.

We crossed hills covered with green coffee bushes. At one of the higher elevations, on a hard turn overlooking the entire valley, there was a small adobe shrine. We stopped and lit a candle while cars slowed down, the passengers crossing themselves as they passed. The view of the valley and mountains to the west was another incredible vista.

We wound up to the top of the mountain and then down the opposite side, catching views of the wide valley east of the mountains and its man-made lake. We then re-joined the Autopista to return to Santiago. The wide, fast road was truly a treat after the dirt mountain roads. Along the side, vegetable and fruit carts were set up, and near the lake fisherman dangled their catch off of long poles, dumping buckets of water on them every few minutes.

On a whim we drove into La Vega for lunch. This is a frenetic city, seemingly designed to get you lost. We drove around looking for their famous church, which guidebooks report as being "generally recognized as hideous." It took us an hour of traversing the matrix of one-way roads before we found the church.

It was indeed ugly. Probably the least aesthetic building any of us had ever seen. As we photographed this monstrosity, a group of children tugged at our shirts and insisted we take their pictures. When we showed them their digital images they hugged us, lighting up the best smiles of the whole trip.

We made our way back to Santiago and found La Siren, a huge store on two levels. The top level had racks of clothes and shelves of non-food items. There was a moving walkway that transported you and your cart between levels, locking the cart wheels on the way.

The first floor was food, from fresh vegetables and meats to canned and other shelf goods to rum and wine. They carried the greatest selection of products we ever came across in the Caribbean. The prices were very reasonable for Dominican or South American products. U.S. name brands were another story. Coffee beans were a particular bargain at $2.50 a pound and of excellent quality.

We used this unprecedented opportunity to splurge. We shopped for three hours, filling shopping carts with vegetables, fruits, cheese, sausages, canned foods, pastas, flour, and much more.

We returned to Luperon with the Suzuki overflowing. We had grocery bags on our laps and stuffed between our legs. There was literally no space for one more bag. We too were stuffed, with fond memories of a unique visit into the mountains of central Dominican Republic.

CARNIVAL

They hold a carnival once a year in Luperon. It was scheduled to begin one afternoon near the end of our stay.

We picked up Charly and Francoise at *Bobato*, and made our way to Letty's for a leisurely lunch. Afterwards we strolled around town. The streets were crowded and everybody was in a holiday mood. Even the young boys carrying guns were smiling.

Late afternoon the festivities got underway. Children ran wild in the streets, announcing the start of the parade. First came young women of high school age dressed in formal gowns. Each was accompanied by a young man in a suit. They were announced as Miss this and Miss that, to lengthy applause and hoots. This went on for a long time. There were a lot of Misses to parade down the street.

The loud crack of a whip startled us. Devils in elaborate headgear sneered threateningly. They ran down and across the street, snapping whips and terrorizing the children. They each had a colorful cloak which flapped menacingly. After they had cleared the streets of evil spirits truck floats arrived.

The first float celebrated the Spanish conquest. There was a naked boy in a grass skirt and three painted black men dancing in cages. The next was a commemoration of the capture of a drug lord. The float was manned by local DEA officials. Bringing up the rear was the heritage float. On this one local officials smiled and waved.

A wood stage had been constructed at the end of the street on the town plaza. Music played loudly from a huge boom-box. We stood through a number of incomprehensible speeches and the crowning of the winner of the Misses. Then, the stage collapsed. There was great pandemonium and several people were hurt. An ambulance arrived and carted off one of the misses whose leg had been broken.

We were later told that the stage had collapsed the previous year and the year prior. Apparently, the town needed a new carpenter.

GLOWING GOODBYE

Chris and Divya gave a farewell concert from the stern of the *Maggie M.* the night before they departed. They had advertised it for a week and we looked forward to the event.

Near dusk a flotilla of dinghies converged on the *Maggie M.* Each tied a line to her stern and then floated back on the current. The mood was festive. Each dinghy brought wine or cocktails. We toasted and chatted and awaited the event.

Chris emerged from below to thank everyone for attending. It was surreal. He was speaking to a flock of baby dinghies tethered to a mother sloop. He asked me to recite a poem I had written about Luperon. I stood up, trying not to tip over, and read the poem. Chris then disappeared below and the suspense built.

After a few minutes he emerged with his guitar. He sat on the stern and launched into a song. He sang and played a number of songs as dusk gave way to night. We enjoyed it thoroughly, toasting each song. Chris had never sounded better. When his set completed he put away his guitar and then spent several minutes arranging lights and a tape player.

With all the drama of a trained MC, Chris then announced Divya. She appeared from below in a formal gown to rousing applause.

Chris fumbled with the tape player and a background orchestra filled the night.

Divya sang opera. The real thing. It was like an outdoor concert in a New York City park. She sang beautifully and loudly and her voice resonated over the water. People anchored nearby came out to sit on their decks and listen. There was wild applause all over the harbor after each song.

After the last song Divya bowed, blew kisses, and thanked everyone. She retreated below. A thunderous ovation brought her back for an encore. Then, a second encore. After the third she finally and regrettably was finished.

We untied our dinghy and drifted away. With an occasional oar stroke to stay on track we rode the current up the harbor. Bright stars shined overhead, illuminating the intensely black night. Suddenly there were flashes of white light in the water around us, like silent fireworks. It was a colony of glow worms, who put on a monthly show based on the cycle of the moon. The females float around, expelling a phosphorescent puddle to attract a male. You can see them swirling in the glow.

It was a perfect goodbye, from Luperon.

Part Two

Dancing with Hurricanes

Charley is coming to Tampa. It is August 2004 and we are living aboard in Sarasota, dangerously close to the predicted path of the expected major hurricane. It would be ugly irony to lose our boat, only months before our planned departure to the Caribbean. We consider running south to Charlotte Harbor, but the storm might deviate from its forecasted path. Anchored out, a hurricane could not only sink our boat, but kill us too. Reluctantly, we leave Nalani *to her fate, and drive to Port Charlotte, to stay with relatives. It is a heart wrenching decision, to leave our home and all our possessions, perhaps to never see them again. Our lives, however, are more important.*

Charley builds into a Category 4 storm off Florida's west coast. He heads up the coast and then unexpectedly jogs east into Charlotte Harbor. Had we gone south we would have been anchored directly in his path. He slams Punta Gorda, wrecking Karin's parents' condo, tearing down electric lines, upending trees, and destroying homes and businesses. We witness the fringes of the storm, flying branches and bending trees, through throbbing windows. Karin's parents, thankfully, had fled to the east coast. Charley continues inland and turns north to rip up the middle of Florida. Nalani *safely rides out a gusty day on Sarasota Bay*

Three weeks later Frances barrels towards Florida. We tie Nalani *in a spider web of lines across a double slip and drive south to stay with friends in Naples. Frances crashes into Florida's East Coast, near West Palm Beach, as a Category 4 storm. She tears up marinas, leaving behind wrecked and sunk boats, and heaving them onto roadways like dead fish. She then careens across the state, passing an hour's drive north of Sarasota. During the raucous night two of* Nalani's *lines chafe through. One of every two boats in our marina suffers damage. Hulls are holed, swim platforms are ripped off, and two boats are sunk.*

Three days later Ivan the terrible, the tenth strongest hurricane on record, devastates Grenada. He runs west to batter Jamaica and whips into Category 5 near Grand Cayman. He is expected to turn around Cuba and barrel directly at us.

We've had enough. We refuse to trust fate a third time. We flee our exposed marina, running Nalani *north to Tampa Bay, where we tuck into the mangroves on the eastern shore at Bahia Beach. We are not out of danger, but we are significantly better protected.* Ivan turns around Cuba and roars east across the Gulf. On the way to Tampa he turns north to Alabama. We are relieved, but shaken.

Two weeks later Category 3 Jeanne crushes Stuart, Florida, and then crosses the state to pass directly over our marina. We ride out 70 mph winds, tending lines as the tidal surge rises several feet over the docks. It is a long, difficult day.

Two months later we set to sea. Ten months after that we would run from another hurricane. This time in the Windward Islands.

BRADENTON
FLORIDA
27° 30' N 82° 35' W

The afternoon of November 10, 2004, we motored out of our marina into the Manatee River at Bradenton, Florida. We were on our way to the Caribbean, taking the first small step of a long journey. An hour later we eased out of the channel to anchor off Emerson Point near the mouth of the river. We had decided to lie at anchor a few days, to gain our sea legs, and to complete last minute boat chores.

We stared at the trees on land to confirm our anchor held, and then shut down the engine. The quiet was overwhelming. Drained by the frantic final days of preparation and fretting over what we forgot, we could not focus on what lay ahead. We were still shaken by the summer hurricanes and fearful of what lay ahead. We had begun our journey, and yet we felt as if we were still preparing for it, not actually doing it.

The moment drifted silently past in the current.

A year earlier we had returned from a four month cruise to the Exuma Islands, including Long Island and Cat Island. That was six years after we had moved aboard our Tayana 37 sloop, *Nalani*.

During those years we had sailed on weekends and short vacations, while we readied the boat for more serious adventures. During the Bahamas cruise we had compiled a list of improvements, which had taken the last year to finish.

We upgraded our power systems with a high capacity alternator, a smart regulator, a wind generator, new batteries, and a small DC/AC convertor. We replaced the wires inside the mast and installed new running lights. For weather reports we added a single-side band receiver and a fax interface to our laptop. We replaced our aging VHF radio with a new model, including a remote control for the cockpit. We installed the latest satellite EPIRB.

We had a canvas enclosure built for the cockpit. It was reinforced with stainless steel ribs and converted the cockpit into an outside room, protected from the weather. On sunny days we could unzip the windows, or remove the top. We added a pedestal guard ahead of the wheel to grab onto, and to hold remote speed and depth gauges. These cockpit improvements made a huge difference in our comfort underway and at anchorages.

We had previously installed a steering wind vane on the stern, to hold the helm under sail. However, we often ran under power, rendering the vane useless. Hand-steering occupies half our crew and compromises safety because it is tiring. To solve this problem we added an electronic auto-pilot, strong enough to steer in storm conditions. We were not disappointed; the auto-pilot quickly earned its way, and we couldn't imagine cruising again without it.

We serviced the engine thoroughly, refreshing all fluids, impellors, and zincs, and replacing hoses and belts. We cleaned and polished and tightened everything. We bought a small outboard for our rowing dinghy and added a removable flotation collar for stability when snorkeling.

This year of preparation included Charley, Frances, Ivan and Jeanne. After the storms had passed we hauled out for fresh bottom paint, and then moved to a temporary slip on the Manatee river in

Bradenton. There, we provisioned and said our farewells. We had enough cash saved to last a year, maybe 18 months. There was more to do, but we had sold our car and had to start sometime.

MARATHON
FLORIDA
24° 42' N 81° 05' W

We spent three days anchored in the Manatee River, unwinding the tensions of departure. We rigged the mainsail reefing system, stowed loose supplies and gear, and lashed water and diesel jugs on deck. We connected the fax interface and tested the new SSB radio, picking up a weather report from Nassau and downloading weather faxes.

Our mood was tense even as we tried to relax. We had not recovered from the pressures of the final week, and I could not shake a sense of foreboding. There was much unknown ahead of us, and the violent storms were still vivid in our memories. It all took a toll on our nerves.

On the third day we ran out of chores and weighed anchor. We crossed lower Tampa Bay to Egmont Key, and then we headed south in the Gulf of Mexico. We followed the coast, staying well offshore in deep water but within sight of land. There was no breeze, so we set the autopilot and ran under power, picking out coastal landmarks and plotting our position. At dusk we opened a bottle of wine and climbed on deck to gaze westward, over the flat water to the horizon.

The sun, fat and yellow, slid into the water, leaving behind a sky painted in yellows and oranges. We toasted and kissed.

Our journey had begun.

That night the wind came up ahead of a cold front. We sailed on the freshening breeze, passing a fleet of shrimp boats, lit up like small stadiums. The next day we made Sanibel Island. The wind had built to a steady 25 knots with higher gusts; the seas were churned up and the swells had become steep. We fought the wind and seas across San Carlos Bay to Naples.

After we passed the protection of Marco Island we were smacked sideways by a breaking wave. It knocked pots on the floor and sent loose instruments and books flying. The seawater that washed over the decks left several fish aboard.

Our course that night would take us offshore as we continued south in deteriorating weather. The seas off Cape Romano are notoriously dangerous in these conditions. We talked it over and decided to turn around and head back north. The wind was expected to shift northeast which would calm the waters near the coast.

We executed a difficult jibe in the strong wind and sloppy seas. A few minutes later another steep wave slammed into our port side, knocking everything below back to the other side. This rattled our confidence, but as we crept north and hugged the coast the wind shifted and the seas settled. At midnight we approached Keewaydin Island, near Naples. We nudged as close to land as we dared and dropped our anchor off the beach. It was remarkably calm in lee of the island. We slept comfortably, happy with our decision.

We lay at anchor the next day letting the front blow itself out. We rested and secured the loose stuff we had not thought necessary to secure. At sea, conditions were rough that day and the next night, but in the lee of our island it was calm and quiet.

The following day the weather settled. We weighed anchor and sailed comfortably in a steady 15 knot breeze under sunny skies. We passed Marco Island again and headed for the Ten Thousand Islands of the Everglades. We anchored off the Shark River. The next day we continued down the coast of Cape Sable and crossed Florida Bay to Marathon. The wind vane steered these days, and we enjoyed the gentle rocking of picture-perfect sails.

We stayed two nights and a day at Marathon Marina where we topped up our tanks, shopped, caught up on emails, and enjoyed dinner with my nephew and his wife who had a home nearby. We then moved into Boot Key Harbor and picked up a City Marina mooring. On the way to our mooring we ran aground and had to kedge off, running an anchor out in the channel with our dinghy.

We stayed ten days in Marathon, waiting for a good weather window. We didn't want to repeat our Marco adventure in the middle of the ocean where the Gulf Stream can raise huge, vertical swells. We explored Marathon, hiking along Route 1 and relaxing in the library.

On Thanksgiving we prepared a traditional turkey dinner aboard, and toasted our thankfulness to each other, to our health, and to *Nalani*.

CHUBB CAY
THE BAHAMAS
25° 25' N 77° 54' W

The Gulf Stream is a wide, wandering river of current that runs north between Florida and the Bahamas. It is notoriously difficult to cross in a small vessel. In practice, if you time the weather properly, keep a good watch for freighters, tankers, and cruise ships, and navigate well, it's not so bad. Weather is critical. Any breeze slightly against the current builds steep waves which can quickly become dangerous. We waited for an acceptable, but not ideal forecast of light SE winds ahead of another cold front.

It took 22 hours, from Boot Key Harbor to South Riding Rocks, where we entered the Bahamas Banks (9 hours under power, 5 hours motor-sailing, and 8 hours sailing). We tracked our progress through the night with the GPS, constantly adjusting our heading against the current pushing us north. We saw our share of commercial traffic, the cruise ships lit up like cities at sea. The seas became steeper through the night; our weather window of calm closed sooner than forecast.

We timed our arrival for dawn. By then the wind had built to a steady 20 knots and the seas were six feet. There was a huge squall ahead of us on the Bahamas Banks. We careened past Castle Rock onto the Banks where we set a double-reefed mainsail and lashed the helm into the wind. Hove-to this way we drifted calmly with the wind, as if at anchor.

Two sailboats followed us onto the Banks. One made the mistake of allowing his auto-pilot to steer through the narrow pass while he videotaped the event. A quick wind shift jibed their main and ripped the sail in half. We watched them limp by under power, as we drifted northeast.

Our original plan was to sail across the Banks and anchor on the east side, near Russell Light. After dawn the next day, we would leave the Banks in good light through the narrow Northwest Channel, and then head across the Tongue of the Ocean to Chubb Cay. However, with the front passing, the seas would be rough and it would be miserable at anchor. We decided instead to stay hove-to and drift all day, napping and relaxing. We would then sail through the night to clear Northwest channel after dawn.

The two boats that had followed us through the pass decided to keep to the usual plan and anchor off Russell Light. It was so rough that night that one of them sheered their anchor rode and drifted away unknowingly. When they awoke the next morning, they wondered why their friends had left without them. They made coffee and relaxed on deck. After a leisurely breakfast they decided to haul up the anchor and discovered to their astonishment that it was they who had left the anchorage early. They were lucky to have not run aground in the shallows.

For us it was a calm, restful day, and a boisterous night sail across the Banks. Our wind vane kept helm duty. The stars came out and a full moon lit our path. After midnight the winds eased, and we shook out a reef, and later switched the staysail for the larger jib. It was a wonderful sail and we were quite happy not to be at anchor, flopping side to side in the swells. We made Northwest channel at dawn.

We arrived that afternoon at Chubb Cay Marina to find it mostly empty. Surprisingly, we were allowed to tie up along an end pier. On previous visits we had to lay bow to the dock, making boarding a gymnastics feat of climbing over the bow pulpit to the bow sprit and jumping to the dock. We hoisted the yellow quarantine flag and waited for the customs agent to arrive from the airport.

After two days at sea the flat still of the protected harbor was luxurious. Relief swept over us, and we basked in a wonderful sense of accomplishment. We had successfully completed another Gulf Stream crossing; we were safely in the Bahamas.

The customs agent arrived and cleared us for an unexpectedly high $300. We happily replaced the yellow Q flag with the Bahamas ensign. We had passed the final trial of our crossing; we were legal and welcome visitors. That night after naps and showers we walked to the marina restaurant to celebrate our arrival. We sat at the bar and ordered rum and tonics.

Charly and Francoise were seated at the bar. They had also cleared in from Florida and were headed to the Caribbean. We introduced ourselves and exchanged stories, quickly forming what would be the basis of a lasting friendship. Reluctantly, we moved to a table, not wanting to part their company, but looking forward to our arrival meal of fresh fish and fried conch. It was delicious.

We slept soundly that night, on calm water.

GEORGETOWN
THE BAHAMAS
23° 31' N 75° 46' W

From Chubb Cay we motored around Whale Cay to anchor inside the cut at Little Whale Cay. We had to stay there the next day because the seas were kicked up by another front passing. The morning after, we broke anchor at dawn and motored across a flat, calm ocean to Rose Island, near Nassau. Our autopilot worked flawlessly, which made the trip an easy ride.

After laying over a night at Bottom Harbor on Rose Island, we headed across the Yellow Banks for the Exumas. Three hours from Rose Island, we heard a loud rattle in the engine room. I immediately shut down the engine and scurried below to investigate. The fan belt had shredded, throwing pieces of rubber and black dust everywhere. Fortunately, we had several spare belts and we were soon back underway. The belt had only 200 hours of use and should not have failed that soon.

We made Shroud Cay that day, one of our all-time favorite anchorages. The next day I removed the alternator and adjusted its position on the engine bracket. It fit better and looked more properly aligned. After a test run to verify the alignment I thought maybe I had fixed the problem. I could not have been more wrong.

From Shroud we sailed to Big Majors Spot, near Staniel Cay. It was a gorgeous sail; the sky was clear blue, there was a steady 10 to 15 knot breeze on our beam, and the seas were flat. We stayed three days and then moved to Cave Cay, to position for a one day run to Georgetown.

We hauled anchor at first light, intending to make the cut off the Banks into the ocean before the tide changed. We missed it by a few minutes. The outgoing tide had already started to run and was kicking up the incoming swells into steep walls. *Nalani's* bow climbed up until we thought she would topple over backwards. She then tipped and crashed down, burying the foredeck under water. She barely righted when the next wave hit.

Karin struggled at the helm, fearful for her life, while I studied the swells and the rocks and shouted directions. It was a frightful few minutes. We seemed to be making no progress and the rocks on each side of the cut closed in towards us. Then the cut widened and the swells eased; we had made open water. We were both shaken. We could have lost the boat and our lives. It was a reminder to never let down our guard.

As we gathered our wits Karin noticed I had put on my shorts backwards that morning. We laughed hysterically, relieving our stress, while *Nalani* set to sea.

We ran south on a fair day over easy seas to Elizabeth Harbor. We studied the charts of the crooked cut into the harbor, and as we entered I checked the GPS against land bearings several times. We made Monument Beach at Stocking Island, where we decided to anchor.

With Karin at the helm I walked forward to deploy the anchor. The chain would not come out the hawse pipe. I went below and climbed over our bed to open the chain locker. The chain was a tangled mess, having been violently tossed about on our way out

Cave Cut. It took me 15 minutes to unravel it while Karin ran *Nalani* in circles.

There were a dozen boats anchored off Monument Beach. Across Elizabeth Harbor in the shallows off Georgetown, 60 boats crowded together. There were another 40 off Volleyball Beach and at other anchorages. The holes were mostly empty. We tried to imagine the harbor in peak season, overflowing with over 500 boats.

Many boaters winter every year in Georgetown. It is a society of snowbirds who gather to renew friendships, and to partake in group events. There are exercise classes, volleyball games, barbeques, yoga on the beach, card games, arts and crafts, sing-alongs, and more. It all ends with the Family Island Regatta. Georgetown is the waterway version of a huge motor home park.

We rode out a front at Monument Beach and afterwards decided to move to Red Shanks, a small, well-sheltered anchorage east of town. We hunkered down there until the end of January, while one winter front after another rolled through. Offshore the seas were whipped up by strong winds and heavy swells. The cuts out of the harbor were impassible.

Bobato joined us at Red Shanks. Each day, after downloading a weather fax and studying the squiggly lines, I rowed over to discuss them with Charly.

"Looks like we'll have a window to get out of here in a few days," I said.

"It's winter," Charly patiently answered. "We have to wait until February." As usual, he was right.

As the days passed, our friendship with Charly and Francoise developed. Charly and I shared a passion for navigation and weather; Francoise inspired us with her energy and cheerful attitude. We exchanged stories and shared chores, and often ventured into town together. Francoise taught us how to make yogurt.

While we waited for the weather to moderate we read books and caught up on email. We received letters and packages from our mail service, and we stocked up from the grocery store in town. We serviced the engine and tuned the rigging. There were many long, wet, dinghy rides over the choppy, wind-driven harbor, loaded down with water and fuel jugs and bags of groceries. A few of the fronts strained our anchor chain in thirty knot plus winds. We fretfully eyed our position, uncomfortably close to a downwind reef. The wind generator often overloaded, making a horrible noise and forcing us to shut it down.

One day I decided to change the gear oil in the dinghy engine. I struggled with a gear pump that leaked, and created an oily mess in the cockpit. Karin got angry and yelled at me. To me, it was nothing unusual: a new task in an awkward position without the proper tools. I could not understand why she was so upset. To her, I was inconsiderate of her home, violating her living space with dirty oil. We had different perspectives and neither of us was completely right. It was an example of how small things can blow up into big problems when two people are confined to a small space. She wrote in her journal that night: "How can you go cruising 24/7 without killing each other?"

We enjoyed the restaurants around Lake Victoria, eating lunches of red snapper and fried conch, and we found amusement in odd places. On a nearby boat, a large, overweight sailor exercised on deck daily, in the nude.

Christmas Eve was calm and quiet; the sunset painted splotches of rose on wispy clouds. On Christmas morning it rained and washed off the decks, and then the skies cleared to a beautiful, bright blue. We were wistful, with no presents and no tree. We went into town to phone family.

Our mood improved when Charly and Francoise arrived for dinner. We had prepared a turkey breast layered with a stuffing of

Mom's bread (a local vendor), garlic green beans, and acorn squash. Francoise brought a pork-stuffed pastry and a Yule dessert: a thin, yellow cake, stuffed with custard and pears, rolled into a log and doused in chocolate sauce. We enjoyed several bottles of wine and a number of new stories. Christmas had come, after all.

On New Year's Eve Karin baked a delicious pizza, topped with squash, spinach, and a pesto sauce. We listened to recorded radio shows from WFMT in Chicago, an eclectic mix of singer song writers. White stars speckled a clear sky.

New Year's Day we rowed over to *Bobato* for a wonderful dinner of savory spinach tart, and pizza loaded with anchovies, blue cheese and onions. There were chocolate covered éclairs for dessert and an apple bread which Karin had baked. With this delicious food, Champagne, and these good friends, we greeted 2005 full of cheer and expectations.

The cold fronts kept coming. January was a month of heavy wind and frequent rain. We settled into a routine of plotting the weather every day and dreaming of calmer days. Meanwhile, we kept up the business of living aboard and whittled down our library of books. Between fronts we explored the harbor in our dinghy and hiked on the unpopulated cays. We strolled the beach at Stocking Island. Mostly we waited, anxious to get moving again. That day finally came at the end of January, like Charly had promised.

GEORGETOWN TO THE TURKS AND CAICOS

We left Red Shanks the morning of January 26. As we motored out the cut by Man of War Cay we had second thoughts. The incoming swells were six feet and looked dangerous. They were not steep though, and we cleared the pass without incident. Outside South Channel Rocks the swells settled and became safely wide. The morning was calm, but our course lay us beam to the swell. We rolled uncomfortably under power to Cape Santa Maria, where we turned north of Long Island and into the Atlantic Ocean.

We planned to sail through the southern Bahamas to the Turks and Caicos in one long run. The path was down the east coast of Long Island to the north of Crooked Island, and then between Samana and Acklins Islands to the Plana Cays and finally Mayaguana. From Mayaguana we would cross the Caicos Passage to the Turks and Caicos Banks and navigate the Sandbore Channel to Sapodilla Bay. We would be alone at sea for two days and nights. This was wild ocean, where many cruisers give up and turn back to Georgetown. We were excited to venture into the unknown, but we were also worried. We would take it one hour at a time.

The first night at sea the moon rose fat and orange. It became too bright to look at, lighting up the sea like a hazy sun. We chugged south under power, taking watch turns with the autopilot at the helm. At dawn a breeze finally came up. We hoisted our sails, and with a grand sense of relief shut down the engine.

We sailed all day on a comfortable beam reach, past Long Island to Crooked Island, where we picked up a boost from a southward current to the Plano Cays and Mayaguana. This was perhaps our loveliest ocean sail ever. The water was purple, the sky blue, and the seas easy. We spotted a pod of whales, blowing and rolling on the surface, and then diving out of sight, tails to the sky. The magnificence of nature was awe-inspiring.

Near Devil's Point, Mayaguana, a fat, roasted sun dipped into the sea. We sat atop the cabin, wine glasses in hand, to witness the huge sphere dissolve into a pool of yellow-orange reflections across the horizon. When the sun succumbed to the sea, a green glow rose in its place, as if marking the spot. We had witnessed the famous green flash for the first time.

Later that night, as we crossed the Caicos Passage, the seas built and clashed against strong and varying currents. We reduced sail and loosened the trim, to slow down. If we moved too fast we crashed into seas from unexpected directions and were tossed about wildly. At under four knots we could pick our way forward, rolling and yawing through the confused seas, in some semblance of order.

At dawn we made West Caicos where we hove-to for the sun to rise. We needed light to read the depths on the Banks. In the Sandbore channel the water was a pure clean blue, even clearer than the Bahamas. We motored up the channel without incident and anchored in Sapodilla Bay. We had made the Turks and Caicos, our first landfall south of the Bahamas.

COCKBURN HARBOR
SOUTH CAICOS
21° 29' N 71° 32' W

We spent four days at Sapodilla Bay, catching up on sleep and touring Provo. We poured over charts and weather maps, plotting different routes to the Dominican Republic. In the end we decided to move to South Caicos first; the weather was too risky to sail directly from Sapodilla Bay. At South Caicos we could ride out fronts and heavy winds, and await a window to run to Luperon.

Our guide books insisted we leave Sapodilla Bay "at the crack of dawn" to venture across the Banks on the Pearl or Starfish Channels. You need good light to read the water, they said, which was chock full of coral heads. You have to arrive at the other side of the Banks in good light. What they don't tell you, is that by leaving so early, you reach the first heads before you can see them. We had several close calls, rejoicing when the sun rose high enough to see clearly.

We sailed a beam breeze dodging the many coral heads across the Banks. We anchored at Middleton Cay because it was getting late. The next morning we moved to South Caicos where we nestled up near the shallow water, deep into Cockburn Harbor.

The weather was deteriorating. A gale with seas over 20' had built north of 27°; a second Low was headed to the central Bahamas from Florida. Luperon was expecting 12' seas out of the north, and highly unusual westerly winds were forecast for the northern Caribbean. Strong winds and heavy seas were headed our way.

Unlike modern and thriving Provo, the village of South Caicos was worn and mostly abandoned. Horses and donkeys roamed the streets. Frightened dogs shied away in the alleys. Litter was everywhere. Many of the buildings were boarded up and most were in disrepair. There was only one grocery store and it was thinly stocked. There were three small restaurants. You had to make reservations, not because they were crowded but to ensure they had food. There was no place to refill water jugs. There was internet access at a private home with two PCs and slow dial-up service.

South Caicos also had its charms. Life was simple and unspoiled. The clocks ran slower, and there were no tourists. The old salt ponds were historically interesting, and the people were quite friendly.

SOUTH CAICOS TO THE DOMINICAN REPUBLIC

We left Cockburn Harbor at dawn, planning to arrive at Luperon during daylight the next day. The forecast was for diminishing winds and seas, which would allow for a safe entrance into Luperon Harbor. We plotted our course from South Caicos to Sand Cay, and then across the ocean to Luperon. This would allow us to stall off Sand Cay if we were ahead of schedule, or to anchor overnight if we were seriously behind. This insurance cost only a few extra miles.

We had a fast sail across the Turks Passage under clear blue skies with dolphins playing at our bow. We reached Sand Cay at noon and hove-to in its lee for lunch. After cleaning up and re-checking our course plots, we set sail for Luperon. Three other boats were transiting from South Caicos to Luperon that day. Among them were Chris and Divya on *Maggie M* and Emil and Olena on *Unicorn*.

That afternoon we lost the wind and it never came back. We had to motor over sloppy swells, flopping and swaying. We raised sail to catch any puffs of breeze, in an attempt to steady the boat. All night the wind would puff and stiffen the sails, and then slack and flap them noisily. The swell rocked and rolled us. The motion and noise made it impossible to sleep.

From time to time we had to alter course to avoid commercial traffic. Intermittently we picked up flashes of running lights or snippets of radio conversations from the *Maggie M* and the boats cruising with them. We tempered our speed to reach Luperon after dawn. It was a loud, rolly, and long night, over a deep and wide ocean.

As dawn broke the mountains of the Dominican Republic emerged, like some distant kingdom.

Part Three

Whales and Pitons

We are crossing the Mona Channel from the Dominican Republic to Puerto Rico. It is our third day at sea and we are under power on autopilot. I am below updating our position plot while Karin stands watch in the cockpit.

"Whale!" Karin shouts.

I scramble up the companionway. We are steaming directly at the middle of a black whale, floating lazily on the surface. The part we can see is bigger than our boat. Karin disables the autopilot and yanks the helm hard right. The whale arches its back, raises its tail to the sky, and sounds, leaving a loud whoosh and a tall geyser in its wake.

We pass by the pool of churned up water and stare wild-eyed. We switch on the depth sounder because we had heard somewhere that whales don't like its pinging. It is a good ten minutes before our heart beats settle.

That night we approach Bahia de Mayaguez on the west coast of Puerto Rico. Overhead, brilliant white stars splatter across a black, moonless sky. The seas are calm and quiet; the thumping of our diesel engine is the only sound. We plan to anchor in the bay to clear customs in the morning.

The black night erupts in a loud roar. We scan the seas for running lights. There are none. The roar rushes towards us and then settles into a rumble, hovering in the dark off our stern. We see nothing. Karin dips below to monitor the VHF. It is silent.

Suddenly it's daylight. We are lit up by a powerful spotlight. I shield my eyes and yell to Karin to hail them. There is no response. She hails again. Still, no response. She tries a third time.

"What was your last port of call?" blares the radio. There is no introduction, no identification.

"Luperon, Dominican Republic," Karin answers. There are a few more questions, and then the night returns. The boat we never did see roars away.

BOQUERÓN
PUERTO RICO
18° 01' N 67° 11' W

Our last day in Luperon we enjoyed lunch at Steve's, and then cleared out at the Inmigración trailer. We hiked to El Commandante's office, finding him relaxed and friendly, dressed in shorts and a colorful shirt. He sent Benjamin to *Nalani* for a departure inspection. Benjamin looked around briefly, and then ordered us to leave the harbor by 5 p.m. We agreed, knowing we would actually stay another night. If we had told the truth, he would have delayed our departure for another inspection the next morning.

After running Benjamin back to town, I cleaned the top half of the anchor chain, hauling up a few feet at a time. It was a long, tedious, and dirty job, scraping off barnacles, oysters, small crabs, and numerous varieties of colorful vegetation. The chain had developed its own ecological system. That night we enjoyed a farewell dinner of Steve's smoked pork chops with eggplant, plantains, and red wine. We were unnerved over setting to sea again. We understood why it was so easy to simply stay. We tried to focus on anticipating new adventures, without dwelling on the hardships.

The alarm sounded before dawn. The bottom half of the anchor chain had been lying in muck. Instead of sea life there were clumps of mud. I dumped buckets of seawater over the links to clean a few feet at a time. Two hours later we finally motored out of the harbor. It was a beautiful sunny day with a light breeze.

Offshore the breeze was dead on our nose, but the swells were wide and low. We motored east along the picturesque, rocky coast of the Dominican Republic. We had enjoyed our time in Luperon, but now that we were past the jitters of departure it felt good to be underway.

We planned to anchor in the protection of a cape for the night, and then continue to Samana the next day. We could then relax a couple of days there and see a new area, before making the run across the Mona Channel to Puerto Rico.

The wind picked up that afternoon. We passed Cabo Macoris, and by the time we reached Cabo Frances it was howling. Anchoring overnight would have been impossible. We hove-to in the lee of the cape for dinner and to await the expected calming at dusk. No such luck. We had no choice but to battle it out and head upwind to Cabo Cabron.

We tacked back and forth all night, motor sailing into heavy winds and building seas. We crashed and bashed and took waves over the bow. It became dangerous. We decided to fall off course to seek some protection from the coast. As we neared the cliffs the seas calmed and the wind became less fierce. Although the diversion cost us six hours, it was well worth the time to be more comfortable and safer.

The next morning we rounded Cabo Cabron and considered running into Samana. Our timing was bad. It was low tide and the wind was strong, whipping up the seas. We were tired though, and the lure of a calm anchorage was strong. We did not want to pass it by. However, we were different sailors by then. We had come together as a team and matured. We discussed the pros and cons of our choices and carefully weighed the risks. We decided the entrance to Samana would be too dangerous in the conditions. We headed offshore instead. It meant another two days and a night at sea. It was not the comfortable decision, but it was the right decision.

The winds settled and the seas calmed while we motored east. We sailed for a few hours, and I took the opportunity to catch up on some maintenance, adding engine oil, replacing the fan belt again, tightening the stuffing box, and seizing a shackle that had come loose on deck. We motored through that night uneventfully.

At dawn we shut the engine down and drifted, to enjoy a quiet breakfast and to take a nap. The rest of the day we motored east. That night (after the whale and speedboat incidents) we made Mayaguez and carefully navigated the harbor to anchor off town. We normally would not have done this after dark, but there was a well marked and wide shipping channel.

The next morning we took the dinghy to town and found customs closed for the weekend. We then had the good luck to meet a local resident who loaned us his cell phone. As U.S. citizens we were able to clear customs by calling San Juan. We then returned to *Nalani* and motored down the coast to Boquerón.

It was sunny and calm when we arrived at the long and wide Bahia de Boquerón. We anchored off the white palm tree beach framed by distant mountains. Jet skies buzzed past us; small fishing boats sliced across the harbor; loud music blared from the beach. We slipped below for a long nap.

Boquerón is a beach village and the party destination of southwest Puerto Rico. On weekends the population overflows, filling the beach during the day and the bars and restaurants at night. During the week, the town reverts to a sleepy fishing village.

Sunday morning we woke refreshed from a wonderfully sound sleep. We took the dinghy to town and walked around, enjoying a lunch of empanadas (fried pastry stuffed with meat) and land-crab rice. We marveled at the culture change: people spoke English, the phones worked, groceries were available, and upscale cars roamed the crowded streets. There was a U.S. Post Office and a variety of shops and restaurants. Stores overflowed with merchandise. Fuel and water were easily available.

We made use of these facilities during the next week to top up our fuel and water, launder clothes, receive mail, catch up on credit cards, and file our tax returns. We changed the engine oil and restocked provisions. As the week came to an end, we looked forward to a vacation.

SOUTHERN COAST OF PUERTO RICO

We left Boquerón and sailed south to Cabo Rojo. This small harbor lies at the southwestern tip of Puerto Rico, which makes it a good staging spot to begin a run east along the southern coast.

Sailing the southern coast of Puerto Rico is a challenge. A stiff east wind builds in the late morning and blows hard all day. The seas build, and the best you can do is motor-sail into it, making only a couple of knots forward progress while you crash and bash and get well beat up. A better strategy is to take it in short hops. If you leave at dawn before the wind comes up you can motor on calm seas until around 10 a.m. At that point, duck into a harbor to await the next day. In this manner, you make easterly progress in short hops. It's all motoring, but there really is no other choice.

We skipped this way from Cabo Rojo to La Parguera, to Cajos de Cana Gorda, to Isla Caja de Muertos, to Salinas, and finally to Puerto Patillas. From there, we turned the corner and crossed to Vieques. This took us two weeks, lying over two days each at La Parguera and Cajos de Cana Gorda, and five days in Salinas.

La Parguera was a small resort town, plagued by jet skis and speedboats. The architecture was picturesque and colorful, though, and there were several good restaurants. There was also an excellent grocery store. We sampled our first "Mo Fungo," which is a delicious mixture of mashed plantains and garlic.

We explored the coastal waters of mangrove cays and quiet bays off the beaten path. We rowed narrow shallow streams under overhanging tree canopies; on one hung a huge termite nest (about four feet high). We ventured to Bahia Fosforescente, famous for nightly shows of dinoflagellates, a marine plankton which flashes when disturbed.

From La Parguera we went to Cajos de Cana Gorda, known as Gilligan's Island. There we found a small, idyllic anchorage, remote from civilization. The bottom was smooth sand and it was protected by a beautiful barrier island with lovely beaches. The walking paths through the mangroves brought back fond memories of the S.S. Minnow and its fearless crew.

We left Cajos de Cana Gorda at 2:30 a.m. A full moon provided plenty of light, and we wanted to make our next landfall before the winds kicked up. Out of nowhere a loud helicopter swooped down and spotlighted us. They hovered for a few minutes with no radio communication and then flew off.

We made Isla Caja de Muertos later that morning and anchored near a hill with a lighthouse. That night a fat, yellow moon rose next to the lighthouse. It was a spectacular sight, as if the moon said to the lighthouse: "You want light? I'll show you light." We left at 3:15 a.m., again using the moonlight for an early departure to Salinas.

Salinas is a cruising destination port. Like Luperon, it has a long, wide, and well-protected harbor with good holding. The outer harbor was lined in mangroves while the inner harbor had houses with grass lawns, landscaped with green palms and large shade trees. Roosters crowed, dogs barked, and song birds tweeted, in a symphony reminiscent of an orchestra tuning up.

The morning sky was wild. To the north, wisps of white clouds and swatches of intense blue hung over sun-dappled mountains. To the south, puffy gray clouds threatened thunderstorms. To the east, the white-hot Caribbean sun burned, but there was still a coolness in the air. Late in the day black storm clouds formed to the southwest, but they never seemed to have the heart for it, and usually dissipated. The air got thick and smelled of smoke.

There was a small village on the harbor with restaurants and shops and a marina with fuel, water, and laundry machines. For more serious shopping the city of Salinas was a long hour walk. There was a bus service, which we used often. Salinas had all the amenities of a city, and access via rental car to anywhere in Puerto Rico. It was a good place to stock up and complete overdue tasks.

We celebrated Easter Sunday with a dinner of ham, baked beans, and yams. The next week we stocked up fresh food and completed maintenance tasks. We changed the engine oil, replaced fuel filters and zincs, cleaned out the head hoses with muriatic acid, caulked the chain plates, and again replaced the fan belt. We rented a car and drove to Ponce, the largest city in Southern Puerto Rico. We toured the Museo de Arte, bought engine oil, and shopped at a WalMart.

From Salinas we went to Puerto Patillias to stage a run to Vieques. The next day we motored along the 12 to 15 meter trench to Punta Tuna with its lighthouse and huge condos built into the hills. There we left the coast of Puerto Rico and headed offshore. We motor-sailed on an easy breeze to the Green Beach on the west coast of Vieques.

We stayed at Green Beach the next day and night, relaxing. We swam in the clear water which turned deep blue offshore, and took long walks along the beach. We witnessed a spectacular sunset across the sea over the mountains of Puerto Rico. A transparent mist shrouded the peaks and above them turned into a mottled gray, then blue, then orange, and then back to gray.

BAHIA ICACOS
ISLA DE VIEQUES
18° 09' N 65°19' W

Vieques lies eight miles east of Puerto Rico. It is 21 miles long and 4 miles wide. In the 1940s the U.S. Navy purchased the eastern and western ends of the island and converted the sugar farms into a sprawling military base. Many local inhabitants were relocated off island, and the rest were moved into the center. The economy, which had been sugar-based, never recovered.

The Navy used Vieques for aerial and naval bombardment exercises until 2003 when the U.S. government succumbed to protests and left. The navy property was converted into wildlife preserves. There were less than 10,000 people inhabiting the center third of the Puerto Rican Commonwealth.

We sailed east from Green Beach along the northern coast, tacking in a light wind over clear, blue water. The green coast rises inland into small brown mountains. We passed Isabel Segunda, with its ferry dock and streets leading up hills to white houses. Two hours later we approached Bahia Icacos, a small, isolated anchorage on the uninhabited eastern tip of the island.

The only evidence of people was an observation tower in the hills inland. Otherwise, we were alone. We stood off the black reefs that hug the bay like protective arms until we spotted the break which leads inside. Carefully, we followed a narrow, twisting path of white sand, through the reef. It wasn't difficult in good light and calm conditions, but it would be impossible otherwise. Once we cleared the reef a small bay opened up, across which was a sweeping arc of white beach. The water was crystal clear and the bottom was pure white. We picked out a nice spot and anchored. The anchor and its chain lay off our bow as if we were floating on air.

We launched the dinghy and rowed to the beach. The sand was fine and pure white. We waded in the water and swam, watching small fish dart in the shallows. The sky and the bay battled for honors of the most impressive blue. We were alone in a small piece of paradise. Off the beach where the bushes and small trees began were signs: "Danger – Explosives." No paradise is perfect.

That night we sat on deck engulfed by thick black with a cloud of fiery white stars overhead. We listened to the waves swish over the reefs.

The next day we snorkeled the reefs. There were mounds of brain coral, and stands of stag and elk horn corals, populated with brightly colored fish. There were lobsters, eels, sea fans, grasses, conch, and sea cucumbers. And, of course, the ever-present barracuda. The water was aquarium clear. We spotted a barnacle encrusted bomb, lying on soft sand in only six feet of water.

Two days later, it was Saturday. Our peaceful anchorage was invaded by four powerboats out of Puerto Rico. They took over our beach with 16 adults, 18 children, and a blasting radio. We decided to flee in our dinghy to inspect Bahia Salinas, the next cove to the east. For this adventure we mounted the dinghy engine, which turned out to be a good choice.

We steered out of our bay and around a small cay where a new vista opened up. Deep blue offshore water broke white on black reefs, and inside the reefs the water changed from a mottled green to brown to white as the depth varied. These waters were framed by a sweeping arc of pristine beach that ended at sheer, white cliffs. We were the sole visitors.

We ran the dinghy to the beach and pulled it up on the sand. We marveled at the natural beauty of pristine nature. Hand-in-hand, we walked up the beach, dipping our feet into the clear water, and admiring the view of changing water colors and white cliffs. To the north, across Sonda de Vieques, was the mist-shrouded island of Culebra. We never looked back, which was a mistake, because we had not anchored the dinghy. We always anchor the dinghy, but we were charmed by the beach, the water was calm, and we thought we had hauled the dinghy sufficiently out of the water. We forgot the tide was coming in and the wind was blowing out. At the white cliffs, Karin looked back and yelled. Our dinghy was bobbing in the swell, floating happily out to sea.

We ran back along the beach, and hearts thumping, splashed out into the waves. The dinghy was by then about 300 yards offshore. I made a quick judgment that I could swim that far and dove. The problem, however, was that I was swimming to a moving object. It was a much longer swim than I anticipated. I crawled, side-stroked, back-stroked, and then crawled again. Each time I looked up the dinghy was disappointingly far away. It always seemed a little closer, though, so I kept going. Karin followed me out to sea, but paced herself more carefully.

I tired and looked around. It was too far to fight the wind back to shore. I had only two choices: catch the dinghy, or, well, I didn't want to think about the second choice. I reassured myself that since the distance to the dinghy was shrinking I would eventually reach it. I side-stroked to save energy. I told myself not to panic. I knew if I were to panic, I was done.

The dinghy kept moving out, but I kept getting closer. Finally, I closed the last few feet, and with an incredible sense of relief grabbed the side of the boat. I was too weak to pull myself aboard. I floated with the dinghy to catch my breath, waving back to Karin that all was well.

I heard waves breaking. We were about to crash onto a coral head. With a surge of adrenaline I pulled myself aboard, started the outboard, and spun the dinghy around. I left the reef only a few feet in my wake. I motored to Karin and hauled her aboard.

We never left the dinghy unanchored on a beach again.

CHARLOTTE AMALIE
ST. THOMAS
18° 19' N 64° 56' W

We sailed from Bahia Icacos across the Sonda de Vieques to Culebra. It was an easy three hour reach on a light breeze, in sloppy seas. It seemed more like a romp across a lake than an offshore transit, with Culebra ahead and Vieques behind, always in view.

We navigated the entrance into Ensenada Honda. The harbor was wide with good depth and wrapped by attractive hills speckled with colorful houses. Fingers of water led to numerous anchorages. We crossed to the west side and anchored off Dewey. The water was calm and clean. It was quiet, but for the occasional rooster and a few planes using the local airfield. Our log showed 1,516 nautical miles (1,745 land miles), since leaving Bradenton, Florida.

We spent a week at Dewey, which is a rustic, small town, with a slow life style. There were several restaurants, a good grocery, and a waterfront bar with fresh water hoses to fill our jugs. Emil and Olena arrived and we took a bus across Culebra to the gorgeous Flamenco Beach: white sand and clear blue water, outlined by black reefs. We enjoyed swimming and walking the beach, and took pictures by the colorfully painted abandoned army tanks, leftover from the days when our military practiced on Culebra.

The day we left Culebra for St. Thomas the sky was blue and the breeze was light. There was just enough angle in the wind to motor-sail on course. Emil and Olena fell behind us, opting to tack under sail. Off Water Island, St. Thomas, we dropped sail and motored up the West Gregerie Channel. Anchored boats lined the shore, in rows up to the edge of the channel. We rounded the northern tip of Hassel Island, passed the Ferry Dock, and crossed St. Thomas Harbor to Long Bay. There we found room to anchor.

The nearby hills were littered with houses and scored with roads. To the south two huge cruise ships lay at dock and another at anchor. A sea plane swooped down and splash-landed to the west. Loud music floated out from town. We rolled uncomfortably on the incoming swell.

We stayed ten days in St. Thomas harbor because I needed a root canal and Karin had a throat infection. We walked the waterfront and the narrow side streets of tourist shops in Charlotte Amalie. We explored the harbor in the dinghy, venturing to Hassel and Water Islands, and Crown Bay. We took a bus to the east end of the island. We visited with friends from Florida who had permanently relocated to St. Thomas. We exchanged dinners and cocktails with Emil and Olena, anchored nearby.

Charlotte Amalie had the largest internet cafe we found anywhere in the Caribbean, and all the amenities of a city. We restocked supplies, including our share of duty-free alcohol. Each night music blared from town making sleep difficult. Our hull amplified the bass booms. We rolled relentlessly on each incoming tide. It was very uncomfortable, and we were overjoyed when the dentist finished his work.

THE VIRGIN AND LEEWARD ISLANDS

We spent a month transiting the Virgin and Leeward islands, from St. Thomas to Dominica. Our first anchorage after leaving St. Thomas was Christmas Cove, Great St. James. After tidying up the boat, we opened a bottle of wine and sat in the cockpit to enjoy the sights. The sights were more unusual than we expected.

An old man emerged from the cabin of the yacht next to us. He was tall and thin, with long white hair and a thick white beard. He was naked but for gray briefs, white socks, and sneakers. He started his engine and then proceeded to haul up his anchor by hand. He would motor forward and then shift to neutral, running to the bow to pull up the slack in the chain. He then ran back to the cockpit to begin the cycle anew.

The process was effective but also quite amusing, given his dress. When the anchor was finally retrieved he moved the boat to a new position and dropped it. After the boat settled he decided he did not like the new position, and the show repeated. This happened three or four times, and then he finally settled back exactly where he had been originally. Satisfied, he shut down the engine and returned below.

The next morning he toured the deck, walking to the bow and back several times. He wore the same socks and sneakers but was missing the briefs.

We cleared into the British Virgin Islands at Jost Van Dyke where we met the rudest government worker of our cruise. We had arrived early and there was no line. I greeted the woman in charge with my officially friendly smile (I had learned the benefit of a smile and a good attitude in dealing with bureaucrats).

"Haven't you ever visited a foreign country before?" She snarled. Taken aback, I stood dumbfounded. I hadn't done anything yet. She offered no clue as to what had offended her. I waited, silently.

"Don't you have anything to give me?" She spat out through an impressive scowl. More silence. We weren't getting anywhere. I had no idea what bothered her. "Your passports?" she finally said, sighing as if confronted by an idiot.

"Oh, sure," I responded. I had them in my hands, but I had learned to not offer anything before being asked. I handed them over. She fumed and stamped angrily, scrawling on a form and then taking my money. When she dismissed me I breathed a sigh of relief at not being thrown in jail for looking perplexed.

We crossed through the BVIs, in short day sails, anchoring each night. The waters were clear and blue; the cays were sparkling white. There was always a good wind. There were nice anchorages, but the bottoms were scoured, rocky, and deep. To solve this, moorings were installed for a daily fee. The restaurants and bars were very expensive, too. Even the price of fuel was high. It was very crowded. In general, we found the BVI's more oriented to fly-in vacationers with holiday money to spend than cruisers on a budget.

We stayed a few days at Virgin Gorda and then set sail east on the Caribbean sea. The currents off Virgin Gorda clashed and made for a rough ride. After dark, the seas settled and the going became pleasant. The stars overhead were beautiful and the Southern Cross rose off the horizon to the south.

After midnight a huge black rock rose on the horizon. It was Saba. There was a towering squall to our north. We risked tacking towards the squall, to stay off soundings and give the Saba Banks a wide berth. They were notorious for piling up nasty seas over shallow waters. Thankfully, the squall dissipated before we got near it.

After sunrise we passed Saba, as forbidding as it was beautiful. Vertical cliffs rose from the sea into steep hills that joined larger hills and small mountains across the entire island. Narrow valleys were nestled inside with swaths of green pasture, looking like fairy tale kingdoms of the middle ages. Swells crashed against the sea cliffs, splashing high spumes into the sky. There were a few moorings in deep water exposed to strong currents and high swells. It was not a place we wanted to tie up.

We passed by St. Eustatius (Statia), which was crowded with oil tankers belching smoke, and ran along the scenic coast of St. Christopher (St. Kitts). There were lush green hills, brown forests, and sweeping valleys of fertile farmland. We anchored at Ballast Bay on the south end of the island. It was a wide, well-protected anchorage, calm and quiet, surrounded by hills of grazing cows. The next morning we crossed the channel to Nevis.

Nevis was charming. There were green and flower speckled hills, good for hiking. The historical town of Charlestown was kept nicely clean, and the architecture, streets, and museums were worth a tour. The people were very friendly.

 We had caught up with Emil and Olena and met them for lunch in town. We then hiked together up a long hill to St. John's Anglican Church. This is the small, stone chapel where in 1787 the famous British Admiral Horatio Nelson married a local widow, Fanny Nesbit. On the walk back to town we toured a building reported to have been the first hotel ever built in the Caribbean. It offered volcano heated water baths, and had bats hanging off electric wires in the ceiling. It was being converted to government offices.

We retraced our path back across the channel to Basseterre, St. Kitts. We wanted to tour the island and to see if we could replace our engine's sea water filter. It was not sealing properly and I had to caulk it every time I opened it to clean. There was no good anchorage, so we headed to the town marina. It had electricity and we were looking forward to an air-conditioning break.

After we docked we discovered our electric cord would not reach the power. No problem – we would simply back out of the slip, turn around, and back in. After forty-five minutes of backing and spinning, we finally maneuvered the stern close enough to a piling to pull ourselves back into the slip. *Nalani* does not back well. We were hot, tired, and frustrated. But the cord fit and we were soon basking in cool air, sipping wine and taking fresh water showers. The luxuries of life. The next day *Nalani* got spiffed up with her first fresh water deck wash in six months.

We hired a taxi who took us to every marine store he knew. Nobody had anything to fix our sea water filter. We gave up and walked into town for lunch. The next day we hired the taxi again, for an island tour. The highlight was the restored English fort on Brimstone Hill. It is built high up the steep hill and the view is spectacular. Our drive continued around the island through plantations and farm land, by small villages and forests with wild monkeys, and past rock cliffs overlooking the ocean.

At the Batik plantation we learned how they color fabric using a unique reverse-dye process. They sketch out a pattern and apply wax where they don't want the dye to take. The material is then soaked in the first dye. After the dye sets the fabric is boiled to melt off the wax. Where the wax had not been is now colored; the waxed areas are clean. New wax is then applied for the next color and the process repeated. The finished cloth is fashioned into dresses and shirts of bright colors and wild patterns.

St. Kitts was the first, and largest, slave market in the Caribbean. There are underground prisons and a network of tunnels under the streets in Basseterre. The town square had served as the marketplace. To this day there is an undercurrent of racial tension which bubbles to the surface frequently. This is not uncommon on other islands, but it was decidedly more open on St. Kitts. Even our taxi driver, an otherwise friendly, and informative guide, lectured us several times on the evils of white people. We could feel the anger well up inside him. After a few minutes the black cloud would dissipate. Still, it was awkward and uncomfortable.

From St. Kitts we crossed to Antigua, and anchored in Five Islands Harbor. We chose it because on the chart it looked like a long, wide, natural harbor, with undeveloped shores. Our initial impression confirmed the chart; it was large and scenic.

We dropped our anchor in a nice 15 foot depth to watch it skid along the scoured bottom. We tried again to the same result. We moved to near Maiden Island and the anchor stuck. I was tired and my back was sore, but we had completed our crossing from St. Kitts. We opened a cold bottle of wine for the sunset.

As soon as we settled in the cockpit, wine glasses in hand, a flock of flies found us. Our idyllic anchorage quickly turned into a nightmare of swishing flies, forcing us to retreat below. The natural, scenic harbor had a garbage dump at its east end. The next morning we motored around the five islands to Jolly Harbor where we cleared customs and took a slip at the marina.

Antigua is one of the richer island nations, with a large number of transplanted Europeans, and a healthy tourist trade. We replaced the leaky sea water filter, taking advantage of the Jolly Harbor boat yard supply shop. The marina had a nice bar and restaurant. Nearby were stores, a bank, and a casino. We relaxed a few days and caught up on land chores. We then sailed south and rounded the coast east to English Harbor.

English Harbor is nautical history; it was the home of Admiral Nelson's fleet. The dockyard has been restored, with shops, bars and restaurants occupying the buildings. The view from Shirley Heights was incredible. From English Harbor we sailed to Guadeloupe.

As we headed down the coast of Guadeloupe, a seabird about the size of a pelican with webbed feet and a long beak crashed through our aft sun screen. He landed on the cockpit locker seat behind the helm, as if to take control. He looked around and eyed us warily, wondering how we got there. He settled down, happy and content, and began to preen his feathers.

We carefully opened the cockpit enclosure to give him an escape path. He had no interest in escape, however. Instead, he appeared to be settling in for a long ride. I grabbed a pillow and approached menacingly. He cocked his head quizzically. I pushed him with the pillow. Instead of fleeing he pecked it. Eventually he realized that the pillow would not give up and he reluctantly flew off.

He circled for a few minutes and then glided towards the cockpit for another landing. I waved the pillow threateningly. Unable to get to the cockpit he changed strategies and landed on the side deck where he strolled to the bow and sat down. Fine, we thought. He'll get bored and fly away. He stretched and preened and curled up, quite enjoying the ride. I had to walk forward and chase him off with the vicious pillow.

The topography of southern Guadeloupe is steep tall mountains. The trade winds funnel through the few cuts, screaming downhill in sudden, strong gusts called williwaws. The day we passed by, on our way to Isles des Saintes, was a brisk sunny day with sloppy offshore seas. We closed to the coast, seeking the protection of land. With full sail up we were struck by a williwaw and knocked down.

Our sails bent parallel to the sea and the rail was underwater. The fuel and water jugs lashed to the gunnels flew overboard and dragged behind us. Books, charts, and tools went airborne below. Even our mattress in the bow was uprooted. It was all quite a mess. Thankfully, all the ports were closed, which was our routine when underway. Had they been open to the breeze, it would have been a wet mess below.

We cut the helm into the wind and quickly dropped the sails. There was no damage done, except to our nerves. We continued on to Les Saintes.

Bourg de Saintes is a colorful hilly French village. We splurged on baguettes, olives, red peppers, salamis, Camembert cheese, wines, and other gustatory delights. There were several wonderful restaurants serving fresh fish and a store that served the best chocolate gelato we've ever had, creamy and beautifully textured.

While in this picturesque village I enjoyed reviving my rusty French. We also hiked up the bluff on the edge of town to Fort Napoleon. Never the scene of any fighting, it houses an interesting museum of Les Saintes, and its grounds have become a botanical garden and home to numerous iguanas.

PRINCE RUPERT BAY
DOMINICA
15° 34' N 61° 28' W

We left Les Saintes, and after swinging our autopilot compass to recalibrate it, had a lively sail south to Dominica. The seas were lumpy and the breeze was stiff; *Nalani* romped like an old race horse feeling her oats. It was fun sailing again. We made Prince Rupert Bay by noon.

The bay is really an indention in land, some two miles long and about a mile wide. It is protected from the north by the Cabrits peninsula. The waters off Portsmouth, in the northern half of the bay, are exceptionally calm. Often crowded, we found few boats with plenty of space. It was clearly not prime time for cruisers at Dominica.

As soon as we turned east into the bay, a skiff ran out to greet us. There is no industry in Dominica, nor any conventional tourist trade. The locals live off farming, or by selling services to cruisers. The latter are called "boat boys." They will watch over your boat, serve as guides, and run errands. Most cruisers adopt one, for fees and tips. They aggressively solicit customers, knowing the first to greet a new boat usually gets the business. We waved the skiff off, saying we planned to use Martin who had been recommended to us.

We anchored north of Portsmouth and south of the Two Turtles Inn. Immediately, we had to wave off another boat boy, and then a third paddled out on a surfboard. He was selling mangoes, and had a basket on his board. We picked out a few fat, ripe mangoes and settled on a price. He paddled off back to shore. The mangoes are, of course, plentiful and cheap in town. But our surfer had demonstrated a different way to skin and eat them, and the demonstration was worth his markup. They were sweet and juicy; our first taste of the fruits of Dominica.

Dominica was wild and undeveloped, appearing much as it must have looked in the 1700's. The only evidence of the modern age were several cargo ship wrecks which had run aground in hurricanes. Nobody had the money or the incentive to remove them. Inland were lush tropical fields and hills and tall mountains. In central Dominica live volcanoes simmered under ancient rainforests, one warming a mountain lake to steam.

We were excited to be there. We felt like truly seasoned cruisers, having reached the end of the Leeward Islands. We were eager to explore the natural beauty of undeveloped Dominica.

The next morning we and five other cruisers met Martin for a tour. We loaded into his van and headed down the coastal road. Not far from Portsmouth, we turned inland and began to go up. Martin's van struggled and the engine whined as we drove along one tight curve after another, heading up the tree-thick mountain. Martin pointed out flowers and herbs growing roadside. Our ears began to pop.

High up the mountain Martin pulled into a parking area. We had reached the Syndicate trail, a long loop through an ancient world of thousand year-old trees. These huge fat monsters sit atop enormous exposed root systems, called buttresses, some the size of automobiles. Many of the roots rise ten feet before merging into the trunk.

There were Gummier trees, seeping a thick white sap, smelling of turpentine, trees with aphrodisiac bark, redwoods, and numerous other varieties. The trail was adorned with vines, ferns, and flowers. Martin showed us orchids, not yet in bloom, several varieties of Birds of Paradise, bromeliads, a Wandering Jew, philodendra, blue wax flowers, and red and yellow heliconias. We were tramping through a rainforest which had evolved over the centuries, untouched by man.

We then drove to a creek bed, which ran through a pasture to a waterfall. We passed banana plants, a nutmeg tree, mangoes, plums, oranges, papaya, and ginger root. There were wild thyme, watercress, laurel, and lemon grass. Martin patiently stopped to point each out and pull samples for us to smell or taste. He explained how locals use the many herbs to treat arthritis, inflammations, wounds, and most other ailments. He was a self-educated naturalist.

At the waterfalls we changed into swim suits and splashed around in the pool at its bottom. The wall of falling water cascading off the cliff was beautiful and loud. I tried to swim through it, to reach the cliff, but the pressure pushed me underwater and I had to retreat.

The next day we again piled into Martin's van, this time for a full day tour. We climbed over inland mountains, thick with trees, vines, and flowers, and descended to the rugged east coast, and the Atlantic Ocean. We stopped frequently to admire the views, of rivers and waterfalls, and of mountain passes. Martin stopped to show us ferns, herbs, flowers, and fruit, which grew wild along the road. We passed through a banana plantation, the fruit wrapped in blue bags for the European market. It was a visual feast.

We picked and ate fresh mangoes, pineapples, passion fruit, star fruit, cherries, and coconut. We saw wild orchids, arrow root, avocadoes, an almond tree, breadfruit, and numerous herbs. Near a nutmeg tree, Martin pointed out a cashew tree. While his attention was diverted I picked a cashew and took a bite. This was a bad mistake. My mouth stung horribly, and I immediately spit it out. Luckily, there was a water pump nearby. I rinsed my mouth several times.

"Don't ever eat a raw cashew," Martin scolded, "Children use them to etch tattoos." Raw cashews are infused with a nasty acid. It took a half-hour to alleviate the burning.

We drove south along the wild, untamed, east coast, with magnificent surf crashing on rocks. We stopped to walk across a field of red rocks, which were actually mounds of hard-packed volcanic dust. Nothing grows on or near them because they contain a high level of toxic metal oxide. They had been shaped by winds and surf. It felt like tramping across a lunar landscape.

We lunched on steamed kingfish and breadfruit at a fishing village, and then visited the Carib reservation, home to descendents of the once natural residents of the Caribbean. We bought a carved wood face, and they gave Karin a basket. The seller threw in a "wife holder" for me. It was a vine laced device that locked a wife's finger to her husband's, to keep her in tow. Karin was not amused.

We headed back west, climbing up into the southern mountains, where we paused at the "Emerald Hole." We followed a trail from the parking lot down a long hill, through dense forest to a lush, green, paradise of ferns, vines, and wide-leaved trees. Nestled inside the blooming green was a clear pool fed by a small, but picturesque waterfall. We dangled our feet in the pool, experiencing what we assumed was the life Adam and Eve had led.

We asked Martin about the boiling lake we had heard about. He explained it was a full day's hike up a rugged trail, high in the mountains. This was not a casual tour, but something you had to train to undertake. It's worth the effort, he said, if you have the time, and the inclination. The lake lies over a live volcano and bubbles with heat, creating a steam cloud. Dominica is a geologically young island and there are several active volcanoes brewing under its mountains.

After we returned to the west coast, we swam across the Lanyoa River to a natural hot water bath, carved out of the river bed. The water is heated by underground volcanic activity. As we relaxed in the steamy water a hummingbird fluttered in the nearby bushes.

At day's end we climbed aboard *Nalani* thoroughly exhausted, but our minds were swimming in floral memories.

Saturday was market day. The open-air market, a cement block with a roof, was filled with tables that overflowed into the nearby streets. We strolled among the tables, taking in the colors and smells, mesmerized.

There were yellow bananas, green plantains, green beans, white dasheen (taro root), purple eggplant, green peppers, red tomatoes, onions, garlic, cucumbers, leafy greens, brown roots; there were piles of fragrant herbs, thyme, lemon grass, and bay; there were baskets of flowers and loaves of fresh bread. Fishermen chopped up mackerel, yellow fin tuna, and dorado to order.

We bought all we could carry. That night we savored a fresh and sweet poached dorado, flavored with thyme and lemon grass, and served with green beans, sautéed plantains, and a cold bottle of Chardonnay. Cruising has its hardships.

The next two days it rained heavily, as a tropical wave moved across the island. We opened our fresh water deck fills and let the rain stream into our tanks. We refilled our spare water jugs, and then every pail and pot we owned. Tired of bailing out the dinghy, we hauled it up and stowed it upside down on the foredeck. The rivers swelled and sent branches, mud, and coconuts into the harbor. It looked as if you could walk from boat to boat, the debris was so thick.

When the weather cleared, Martin took us up the Indian River in his skiff. This is a highly advertised tourist trip, a "must see" of any visit to Dominica. The river was picturesque, and we were amused by land crabs skittering over tree roots. However, the river was muddy from the rains, and after our other trips with Martin this felt more like canned tourism. Even Martin was bored, simply going through the motions. At the upriver end of the trip there was a house offering rum drinks and selling tourist memorabilia. It was too predictable.

LE MARIN
MARTINIQUE
14° 28' N 60° 53' W

We sailed across the Martinique channel from Dominica to St. Pierre, at the foot of Mount Pelée, where we anchored on the narrow shelf which hugs the coast off deep soundings. In 1902 Mount Pelée erupted and destroyed the town, killing over 30,000 people. There were only two survivors, one of which had the good luck to be in jail that morning, the only safe place in town.

We rolled all night and were happy to escape in our dinghy to town the next morning. We strolled through the French village, admiring the architecture and finding a Boulanger (bakery and cafe) for baguette sandwiches. In the town center there was a small, clean, open-air market, where we bought avocados and a red snapper for dinner.

After lunch, we hauled anchor and motored down the coast of Martinique to Grande Anse d'Arlets. The town sits inland on a wide harbor, nestled in the mountains of southwest Martinique. There was plenty of room, and the water was clean and clear. To our joy, it was also flat calm. The town itself is a charming strip of colorful houses. We lunched the next day at a small restaurant on Brochette des

Lambis (grilled skewers of Conch) with Biere Loraine. I struggled with my inept French but enjoyed using it.

The next day we left Grande Anse d'Arlets and rounded the south coast. We passed by St. Anne to enter the huge harbor, Cul-de-sac du Marin. There were literally thousands of boats in the harbor, 600 inside one enormous marina. Marin is the yachting capital of Martinique, if not all of the Windward Islands. After we anchored, we launched the dinghy to visit the town.

Hungry, we spotted a food shack labeled "Poulet Roti." I knew poulet was chicken, and we had heard about the roti sandwiches of Trinidad. I stepped up and proudly ordered in French: deux (two) poulet roti. There was some confusion about how I wanted them prepared, and my faltering French failed me. Pour dejeuner (for lunch) I managed, and pointed to plates. The server shrugged and picked up two whole chickens. I had ordered two roasted chickens. I quickly changed our order to one, mostly using frantic sign language. It was a lunch of plain roasted chicken, but it was delicious.

We walked to a nearby grocery store. The shelves were filled and there was a wide selection of French cheeses, wines, pates, ham, salamis, and, of course, freshly baked baguettes. Vive le France.

We ate well at Marin, taking the dinghy into the marina for a breakfast of chocolate croissants, and enjoying lunches at the many restaurants. We used the calm harbor and the availability of nautical supplies and services to catch up on numerous boat chores. Karin cleaned the stove while I spliced a new dinghy painter. We upgraded our electronic auto-pilot by downloading new software.

One day we rented a car with another couple and toured the island. We visited the Musee de la Banane, where we learned there are some 300 varieties of bananas, 44 of which were on the grounds. There were huge, fat bananas, the shape of gourds, and tiny bananas curved like bird beaks. We watched the cleaning and boxing of bananas for shipment.

We then traveled to the Saint James Distillery, where we witnessed the process of making rum. First, sugar cane is chopped up and mashed with water. The mash is fermented in huge vats with yeast. When fermentation is complete the liquid is distilled through large columns of condensing plates, and then stored in stainless steel drums or oak barrels to age. Empty bottles are trotted out on a belt to a machine which fills and tops them.

Most of the rums bottled on Martinique are Rhum Agricole, which are made from sugar cane juice; most commercial rums are Rhum Industriel, which are made from molasses. Rum is controlled by the French Appellation Controllee laws, the same as wines. The best rums are sipped and valued like a good cognac.

From Saint James we drove up the west coast, passing garden-like farms, banana plantations, sugar cane crops, and small villages. It was pristine with lush tropical flowers everywhere. We then crossed the northern mountains to the east coast. There were steep climbs through rain forest, along sheer drop-offs to stream beds far below. The winding roads were meticulously maintained. Compared to the raw natural beauty of Dominica, Martinique had the look of a cultured garden.

RODNEY BAY
ST. LUCIA
14° 05' N 60° 58' W

We left Martinique the morning after a Low passed and the day before another was due. The winds were up, the seas roiled, and the skies cloudy. We set a reef in the main and flew the jib. *Nalani* loped over four to five foot seas, happy to be at sea again.

Half way across the channel to St. Lucia the winds increased. I climbed on deck and took in the second reef. I was hardly back in the cockpit when a squall hit. The winds howled to 40 knots while clouds swirled overhead and rain flew sideways. *Nalani* stiffened and crashed forward into confused and building seas.

I cut the helm into the wind to reduce the force, being careful not to turn too far, which would flap the sails violently and possibly rip them. For thirty minutes we ignored our heading and followed the wind as it swept the compass. When the storm passed and the seas settled, we resumed course to St. Lucia.

We made the northern coast and turned into Rodney Bay. When safely inside we dropped our sails and motored across the bay. We took a slip in the Rodney Bay Marina and cleared customs. Charly and Francoise were there with *Bobato*. They joined us for a beer and a baguette sandwich at the marina cafe.

It was late June and hurricane season had officially begun. Lows were forming frequently, and with them came thunderstorms and heavy rains. We considered riding out the season at Rodney Bay Marina. It is one of the best protected marinas in the Windward Islands. St. Lucia, however, lies in the active storm latitudes. We postponed our decision, since the early tropical storms usually formed west of the islands.

The marina had an internet cafe, a bank, a chandlery, a small grocery store, a liquor store, two restaurants, a laundry, and convenient trash disposal. There was a boat yard next door, and a conventional hardware store a short walk away. Transportation was convenient and cheap on vans called "maxi-taxis." They run up and down the island, and you can get on or off anywhere along the way. We never had to wait more than a few minutes for one. At our slip we had piped water and electricity. We could run the air-conditioner. This was luxury.

Charly flew to France to visit family and while he was away Francoise offered to show us Castries, the capital. We flagged a maxi-taxi outside the marina which dropped us off downtown.

Castries is a crowded city and the streets are busy with traffic. We walked across town, passing about a hundred shoe stores, to an old church, remarkable because its entire interior is painted in artistic scenes – walls, ceiling and windows. We made our way to the large downtown market where vendors hawk clothing, fruits, vegetables, spices, herbs, meats, and fish.

We wandered through the market, stopping at one table after another, happily filling our knapsacks. At the fish stands, we bought a plastic bag from one vender, a small tuna from another, and then paid a third to clean and pack the fish. On the way home, as we sat in a crowded maxi-taxi, I worried that the bagged tuna on my lap would leak. It didn't.

That night I cut out the bones, skin, and blood red meat, and fried the remains in olive oil with garlic, onions, and Cajun spices. I pressure-cooked a breadfruit as a side dish. Karin served fresh bread with olives, artichoke hearts, avocados, and cheese. Francoise donated two bottles of Cotes-de-Rhone, and we ate happily and heartily. For dessert we sipped St. James rum and told each other stories.

The next day, barely awake and hung over, we noticed a skiff moving boat to boat along our row. It was covered in a tent of colorful flags, draped off a makeshift mast. Gregory grabbed our stern rail and waved. There were piles of fresh fruit spread over his floorboards. We bought a papaya, a few mangoes, and some avocados. Gregory was a marina fixture and stopped by almost every day. Once we settled into a shopping routine we had no need of him. We occasionally bought from him anyway due to his perseverance.

We buckled down to work long deferred: waxing the topsides, cleaning out the water tanks, and servicing the wind generator and dinghy engine. We again flushed out the head pipes with muriatic acid. I found an electronics store and bought a connector for our laptop. This allowed us to download another version of our autopilot software. It was a true work-in-progress.

When Charly returned from France we took a taxi tour of the island. The first stop was a scenic overlook of Castries, high up a hill at an old fort. The fort had been converted into a community college, but cannons still aimed out to sea from beautifully manicured lawns.

We then wove south along the coast, stopping to admire Marigot Bay, a postcard-perfect anchorage of azure-blue water, tucked into beautifully green hills. We passed a man walking along the road carrying a boa constrictor. Our driver was a mango aficionado, and he lectured on the flavors and sweetness levels of his favorite twenty varieties. He pulled over at several trees, to let us to sample the delicious fruit, dripping juice down our faces.

"Why are there so many shoe stores in Castries?" I asked at one point.

"They's a lot of feets on St. Lucia," he observed, flatly.

We continued south, climbing up hills through rainforest and curving past overlooks with spectacular views of the Caribbean Sea. We pulled off the road several times for glimpses of the famous Pitons, which dominate the landscape of St. Lucia's southwest coast. These two rock mountains are shaped like steep cones. They are volcanic plugs, a distinct geological phenomena, and a marvel to view. At their feet is a live volcano.

We descended into Soufriere, and then back up into mountains, where we parked in the bowl of the volcano. Sulfur steam wafted from pools of iron-oxide mud, bubbling at 300° F. Although the volcano last blew in the 1700's, we could not shake a feeling of unease.

From the volcano we drove back up one of the mountains to the Ladera Resort for lunch. The resort is built into the side of the mountain. We ate lunch by the pool, which is set on the edge of a sheer cliff, giving the appearance of flowing off into thin air. Our table overlooked both Gros and Petit Pitons, and the sea between them. It was a spectacular view. Charly and I picked up water pistols meant to scare off birds and shot at each other.

After lunch we drove to the botanical garden at Diamond Falls. The garden is a well-manicured lawn with paths through cocoa trees, rainforest plants, flowers, and fruits. The falls are pretty, but by then we were tiring of falls.

When the taxi dropped us off at the marina we were dog-tired, but thankful the tour had showed us so many colorful images of St. Lucia.

We stayed three weeks at Rodney Bay Marina, completing boat projects, shopping, and doing laundry – the stuff of daily cruising life. Tropical waves passed over us dumping rain and warnings.

Part Four

Steel Music and Shark Bake

The night of July 10, 2005 a tropical wave in the eastern Atlantic coalesces into a depression. The system is expected to turn north as it moves west, and pass over Martinique. It may strengthen into a tropical storm. We are at Rodney Bay, St. Lucia. If the storm wanders below its projected path and gains strength, we could be in the wrong place at the wrong time. Our memories of the Florida hurricanes are still strong. We decide to run south, to safer waters.

We clear customs, top up our diesel, and motor out into Rodney Bay. The sky is deceptively blue and the seas are calm. Whatever breeze there is, is blocked by the land. We run down the coast, passing the Pitons, standing guard. As we clear the lee of St. Lucia, a westerly wind builds and we hoist sail.

We had planned to sail through the night, down the west coast of St. Vincent to Bequia. We decide instead to keep moving south, beyond the Grenadines, to Carriacou. We want more distance from the storm path and Tyrell Bay is a large and well-protected anchorage, where we could ride out any outer-band weather.

At midnight we clear St. Vincent and the wind ratchets up. We switch from autopilot to wind vane. We romp south on a lively sail, reaching Carriacou the next morning. Tyrell Bay is crowded but we find a spot to anchor. We look forward to a good rest in the safe harbor.

As we deploy the dinghy to clear customs we overhear a VHF conversation. The depression has strengthened into Tropical Storm Emily. Her path has been revised southward ... to Carriacou.

RUNNING FROM EMILY

We had just anchored in Tyrell Bay, Carriacou, when we overheard that Tropical Storm Emily was headed there. Howard, on the trawler *Serendipity*, stopped by to introduce himself. He said he planned to tie off in the mangroves and ride it out. Later, we overheard him on the radio speaking of "getting out of harm's way."

We decided to run. Knowing it could be rough at sea we precooked a few meals and ate lunch. We then weighed anchor and headed back out of Tyrell Bay. We sailed south along the coast of Grenada, and discussed tucking into a harbor on Grenada's south coast. I took a nap and Karin showered on deck with our converted bug sprayer. The seas were easy, and the wind was steady and gentle.

As the sun set we received an Emily update. She was expected to strengthen into a hurricane, and her course was revised south ... to southern Grenada. We set course for Trinidad.

That night the breeze disappeared and the seas settled. Overhead, the stars were bright. The eerie calm hinted at impending danger. We motored south over ominously flat seas, wishing the storm to turn north. At midnight we were midway between Grenada and Trinidad in the open ocean. Emily's track was revised, yet again. She was now expected to pass ... midway between Grenada and Trinidad.

An alarm sounded. I quickly shut the engine down. We bobbed powerless, without a whiff of wind. The current pushed us west in the thick black of the moonless night. Emily was bearing down. We worked to hold back the fear curling up in our bellies.

I opened the engine room. There was black dust everywhere and the fan belt was shredded. Methodically, I removed the debris and installed a new belt, thankful for the spare. The engine started and we were back underway.

Two hours later there was a loud rattle. I shut down the engine again and scurried below. The new fan belt was ripped apart. Now, I really worried. We were floating helpless in dead calm in the path of a hurricane.

I aimed my flashlight and studied the engine. Why did the belt break? Did I over tighten it? Is the alignment off? What went wrong? I checked off each possibility and found nothing amiss. Then, I spotted a piece of a fan belt, about the size of a dime, wedged into the engine pulley. I cleared it and methodically inspected the other pulleys. I installed another belt. The engine started and we were underway again.

I cut our RPMs by a third. We lost some speed, which was not good with a hurricane approaching, but I didn't want to stress the engine and risk more problems. Emily refused to turn north. We chugged south, frightened.

Dawn broke and revealed the coast of Trinidad ahead. We had three problems. First, since we had not planned on visiting Trinidad we had no charts. Second, we had to fight a strong outgoing current in the Boca de Monos to get to Chaguaramas harbor. If we lost the engine we would be flushed out to sea, helpless. Third, Emily's track had been revised again. She was now heading ... directly to Trinidad.

We navigated the Boca de Monos with our hearts in our throats. I kept the RPMs only high enough to make slow progress. We watched water rush by our hull while we only crept past land. We urged the engine to keep running. Finally, we cleared the cut and turned into Chaguaramas Harbor.

The harbor was deathly quiet. All the moorings were taken. There was no safe place to anchor. We hailed several boatyards on the VHF. Nobody had room. They were filled and hunkered down for the storm. We were out of options.

"*Nalani, Nalani*, this is *Unicorn*."

Emil's voice was like a lifeline thrown to drowning victims. *Unicorn* was anchored in Carenage Bay, on the other side of a hilly outcropping of land, south of Chaguaramas. Emil piloted us over the radio around the land to the harbor. It was well protected, except from west to south, but the strong winds would be out of the east and north.

We motored into the harbor. We had been on the run for 52 hours and we were tired and scared. We dropped our anchor and a nearby boat yelled at us, claiming we were too close. We anchored a second time to more yells, and then a third time. Each move took us farther away from the protection of the hills. By then, we were frantic and exhausted; Karin burst into tears.

We stowed sails below and stripped the decks of loose items. We tied down whatever we could not bring below. We let out all our anchor chain and 20 feet of nylon rode. We decided not to deploy a second anchor, since we were unsure of wind direction. We readied the second anchor, however, to drop on a moment's notice.

Emily was three hours away.

CHAGUARAMAS
TRINIDAD
10° 41' N 61° 38' W

After crossing Tobago, Hurricane Emily veered north and slammed into northern Grenada and Carriacou with 90 mph winds. Two hospitals flooded and over 200 homes were destroyed. Emily left behind over $100 million in damages, less than a year after Ivan had wrecked Grenada. We learned that *Serendipity* was sunk in the storm and Howard had floated at sea for 15 hours before being rescued.

We fell asleep in the salon that night, monitoring radio updates on Emily's track. Protected by the hills around Carenage Bay and with the center passing to our north, we had breezes of only 20 knots and a few gusts of 30. *Nalani* hardly rocked and we slept soundly, exhausted from our run.

The next morning we were jolted awake. *Nalani* pitched and rolled, and dishes and pots rattled loudly. We staggered up lurching stairs to the cockpit. Four and five foot swells were rolling into the anchorage. The winds on the backside of the storm had shifted westerly and were blowing unchallenged across the Gulf of Paria, building seas and driving them into our anchorage. Like a frightened horse, *Nalani* bucked and reared and tugged at her anchor. The incoming swell brought mud, bark, branches, logs, and plastic bottles.

We dropped our second anchor in place and prepared its line to run out, in the event we lost our primary anchor. This was a calculated decision, as two anchors out would complicate re-anchoring. However, we had plenty of room to drag and the bottom was good. We thought it more likely the second anchor would bite and hold, if the first failed.

For the next six hours we rocked and rolled and kept a watchful eye on the anchor, letting out rode regularly to prevent chafe. Three boats dragged across the anchorage but *Nalani* held her place. Hours later the wind shifted south and then east of south. The swell settled. We were safe at last.

Emily grew into a fierce category 5 storm with winds of 160 mph, the strongest storm ever recorded in July. She brushed Jamaica, causing severe landslides, and then smacked into Cozumel, Mexico, wreaking havoc on the Mayan coast. She then weakened and wobbled north into the Gulf of Mexico, where she regained category 3 strength and made a second Mexican landfall. As we followed the progress of this dangerous storm, we recalled with a chill how we had bobbed powerless out in the ocean, so close to her eventual path.

A week later we left Carenage Bay for Chaguaramas Harbor, where we had rented dockage at Tropical Marine. Each boat was allocated a small space along the dock to lay bow or stern to. We picked up a mooring for our stern and maneuvered bow-first into our tight space. We were between another Tayana 37 and a marina skiff. We tied bow lines to the dock, secured the stern mooring, and set fenders on our sides.

To disembark, we had to climb over *Nalani's* bow pulpit, step on the bow sprit, and jump to the dock. This was quite a feat at high tide. After checking in, we hooked up electricity and set a stair box at the bow. This was an improvement over jumping, but we still had to climb over the anchor and the bow pulpit. This made loading groceries and other supplies difficult, to say the least. However, we had a home to ride out hurricane season.

Chaguaramas Harbor is ringed by boatyards: Crews Inn, Tropical Marine, Coral Cove, Power Boats, Peakes, and IMS. Each has wet slips, one or more restaurants, and retail shops. All but Tropical Marine and Coral Cove have haul-out yards. In and around the yards are welders, riggers, hull painters, carpenters, mechanics, teak shops, canvas shops, sail makers, chandleries, and more. You can find any part or service you might need, at substantially lower cost than anywhere we'd been. The restaurants vary from the expensive Crews Inn overlooking the harbor to the Roti Hut, serving wraps of curried goat meat with bones from a trailer in the bushes.

Tropical Marine ran a wholesale fishing and export business. The freezer overflow provided a steady stream of meals for their restaurant. We frequently ate fish for lunch and it was always good. On Friday nights they served a popular barbeque of fish, chicken, and ribs, with sides of salad and rice. Cruisers gathered and swapped stories over cheap beer.

We attended our first barbeque the week we arrived. After dinner a local steel drum band stopped by to practice and entertain. Steel drums are the musical invention of oil workers. The top of an oil drum is pressed inward and stretched, forming a bowl. A paper template is then used to etch a circle for each note in its proper position on the bowl. These circles are banged outward into bubbles on the bowl's surface. Each bubble is carefully shaped to sound a perfect-pitch note when tapped.

That first night we listened to a lively rendition of *Amazing Grace* performed on six drums, and a beautiful *Over the Rainbow* solo by the band's leader. Steel music was a national obsession and pleasant to the ears, sounding something like the offspring of a flute and a harpsichord.

Tropical Marine had a lively social atmosphere. We regularly visited other boats, and each week there were two tournaments at the outdoor tables of the restaurant: Mexican dominoes and bridge. Dominoes usually attracted a crowd of 15 to 20 players and observers. As the tiles clicked on the tables stories were exchanged, plans for trips made, and shopping tours arranged. The winner's prize was weekly bragging rights.

Bridge was more serious. Each player paid a fee and the winner took all, save a small hold-back to buy cards. If you won you could buy yourself lunch and a couple of beers. More important, was the recognition. Some very good bridge players showed up, including two locals who regularly played in professional tournaments. The cards were dealt in serious quiet.

We played dominoes most weeks but eventually tired of it. I had played bridge years ago and happily resumed my apprenticeship. I bought a couple of books to refresh my memory and to study new skills. You have to count points to assess the strength of your hand, and then participate in bidding, trying to communicate with your partner while not giving away the store to your opponents. Then there is the strategy and tactics of playing out the hand. I studied seriously and trained with a laptop bridge program. Each week I improved, and near the end of our stay I won the tournament two weeks in a row. That fluffed up my feathers.

THE ENTREPRENEUR

There are many entrepreneurs in Chaguaramas. They varnish wood, polish hulls, clean decks, and fabricate rails; they sell fish, do rope work, and run taxi services; they shop for you. They are the carpenters, painters, mechanics, and sail makers. Many are do-anything assistants.

"I'm the guy who cleans boat bottoms," announced a smiling Trini one day. I was crawling over the bow pulpit on my way somewhere. "I do a good job. I clean all the boats here." That meant that maybe he had once cleaned a boat in the marina.

"I don't need any help," I answered.

"Yes mon, this water is bad. I'm the guy who will clean for you." He began pulling off his shirt.

"No, not today," I insisted. He shrugged and wandered off.

Almost every day a different entrepreneur would stop by and announce: "I'm the guy who ..." They were all friendly and talkative, and they all had a distinct hearing problem with the word "no." After trying friendly "no thanks" several times you had to be rude to get them to give up.

Of course our hull did need attention, and I had no interest in swimming in the harbor muck, so I eventually negotiated a price with our entrepreneur. He immediately stripped to his underwear.

"You have a face mask?" he asked. "And, some kind of scraper?" This from the guy who "does all the boat bottoms around here."

"No, I don't have anything you can use," I answered, perturbed. I did not want my mask to be lost, or broken, and I felt, perhaps unreasonably, that a boat bottom cleaner should have his own scraper. He shrugged.

"I be back, mon," he said, pulling his shorts back up.

Two days later, true to his word he returned with a mask and a scraper. He had borrowed them from some other boater. He stripped again, leaving his shorts and shirt in a pile on the dock, and jumped into the water. He scraped at the water line and then relaxed, floating on the surface. He chatted with passersby. I reminded him to clean the barnacles off the prop.

"Oh yes," he assured, holding up a plastic grocery bag. "Bag da prop and nothing grow." He scraped some more and then floated around again. When he finished at least the water line looked clean.

Every few weeks he returned for another go at it. He learned to borrow a mask and scraper before he showed up. I knew that without flippers, weights, or any air-supply, he could not be doing much of a job, but it saved me from the oily water.

There were many entrepreneurs in Chaguaramas, each ready to attack some task with glee. To be fair there were many good workers, but you had to be careful.

THE MECHANIC

The mechanic was a large man. He stood over six feet tall and weighed more than 250 pounds. We had hired him to fix our alternator belt problem.

He liked to tell stories and he preferred to remove things from the engine to fix them elsewhere. This was because he often had the repair done by somebody else, and because he didn't fit well in our engine room. He fussed with the alternator and belts, adjusting this and that; he replaced a pulley and inserted spacing washers. It was fixed, he announced.

He then overhauled our sea water cooling system, and while at it, he discovered that our engine mounts needed replacement. The latter required disconnecting the prop shaft and raising the engine with a block and tackle. This was not for the faint hearted, but after inspecting the mounts I agreed it was necessary.

He arrived one morning and got to work. He removed our cockpit stairs and dangled a block and tackle from a 4x4 set across the hatch. He hooked it to the engine, unwound the mounts, and hiked up the block. We now had an engine suspended in our cabin, no stairs, and a block and tackle hanging in the companionway. To leave the boat, we had to climb on the sink, slink around the tackle and board, and haul ourselves into the cockpit. Returning, we had to repeat the gymnastics in reverse. This was a bit more difficult than climbing over the bow pulpit to the dock.

The mechanic inspected his work and was pleased. Then he announced he had to run an errand. He was always leaving to run errands; sometimes he came back, sometimes he didn't.

"What do we do until you return?" I asked.

"Yeah, well, don't knock the rig about. It should be fine."

He returned two days later. Since it was Friday he couldn't finish up until the next week. It wasn't until late Tuesday that the job was finally done and the engine dropped back in place. We had stairs to the cockpit once again.

After the mechanic was gone I studied the alternator. It still didn't look right. I removed the alternator and its pulleys, and carried them over to a local alternator shop.

"The pulleys are different widths," the owner observed. "No belt will ever work right." He exchanged the odd pulley for me, and then I reinstalled everything. It looked great and the alignment was perfect. In fact we never had another problem with alternator belts.

Pleased with this process I removed our starter motor, which had begun to act up, and brought it to a starter repair company. It was overhauled, greased, and cleaned up.

To the mechanic's credit, we had no further problems with the water cooler or the engine mounts.

TURTLE BABIES

Jesse ran a business called "Member's Club" out of an office at Tropical Marine. He shuttled cruisers to events of interest, offered island tours, and ran weekly shopping trips. On Saturdays he took groups to the Central Market in Port-of-Spain. These trips were coordinated over the VHF, which served as a cruisers' party-line. Jesse employed a network of locals who provided their own cars and vans. This allowed him to expand or contract the business, as necessary. He was friendly and competent, and most cruisers came to rely on him.

Each year leatherback turtles migrate to a beach at Matura Bay on Trinidad's east coast. They come to lay eggs. During this time Jesse runs weekly trips to observe them and the mad scramble of hatchlings to the sea. Locals patrol the beach to protect the turtles from poachers who used to slaughter up to a dozen every night.

We left one afternoon with Emil and Olena and a handful of other cruisers, including two children. As we drove through Port of Spain in his van, Jesse pointed out the sights and related Trinidad history. Like other Caribbean islands, sugar cane farms imported African slaves. When the slaves ran out, they recruited East Indians at slave-like wages. Today, the population is 80% Black and Indian, with the remainder about 15% Oriental and 5% European. The business class is mostly Indian, while the bulk of the workers are Blacks. There is a constant clash for power among these two groups with over 200 kidnappings a year for ransom.

As we approached Matura Bay, Jesse switched his narration to the habits of the Leatherback Turtle. They travel years and thousands of miles at sea, eventually returning to the same beach on which they hatched. The egg-laying has become a local festival, protected and controlled by an organized force of volunteers.

At Matura Bay we disembarked and gathered in a gazebo to await a radio call from the beach. It was all well organized; they don't want people roaming the beach and frightening the turtles. Jesse served cheese sandwiches and fruit juice as night descended. Two hours later his mobile phone rang. A nest of hatchlings were emerging. A guide arrived to lead us to the beach.

A nest of baby turtles had dug themselves out and were crawling around on the sand. There were dozens, each small enough to fit in your hand. They scattered in all directions, swimming on the sand with tiny flippers. They head for light, since the sea is lighter than the land. One guide demonstrated with a flashlight. Wherever he aimed the light the turtles chased it. When all the flashlights were switched off, they got their bearings and headed for the sea.

Some would be picked off by birds before they made the water. The rest swim directly offshore for several weeks without pausing to feed or rest. They get their nourishment from leftover egg yolk carried in a sack under their belly. All but one in a thousand succumb to predators, or other misfortunes. That one survivor spends an average of 25 years at sea before returning to the same beach to lay her first eggs.

As we watched the baby turtles, a large female was arriving from the sea. We were carefully gathered together and led up the beach to observe her. This would be one of a dozen nests, each with about 50 eggs, she would make every two weeks over the summer. She would then leave for a few years before returning to nest again. Our mother was about six feet long and weighed a ton. We were told she was small; many are double her size.

She shuffled inland onto the soft sand and began excavating a hole with her back flippers. She dug with her left flipper while using her right flipper to tamp the sides. She then shifted and dug with the right flipper while packing sand with the left. In this manner she steadily dug a hole two feet deep and a foot wide. When she was satisfied with the hole she went into a trance and began dropping eggs. During this time we could light our flashlights, take pictures, walk around her, even pat her shell. Nothing broke her trance as she continued to drop eggs.

After the last egg dropped she slowly came out of her trance. Our guide instructed all lights off and swept us back, to give her space. She got to work immediately, filling up the hole with sand. She then shuffled along the surface tossing sand in the air, tamping it with her flippers, and roughing it up with her belly, all to conceal the nest. When she was done she lumbered back to the sea, leaving behind no sign of the nest.

We were stunned. We stood speechless in awe of the power and intelligence of nature. We were grateful to have witnessed such a spectacular event, but we also felt some voyeuristic remorse. However, our presence was not harmful and certainly better than the killings, which used to be routine. The community had showed courage in keeping out the poachers, and we were a replacement source of income. For that we applaud them.

MUSICAL FOOD

The cuisine of Trinidad is as varied as its music. There are African, Indian, and Oriental dishes, and invented combinations. Good fish, fresh vegetables, and wonderful fruit, like sweet mangoes abound. Below are a few unique dishes we particularly enjoyed.

Doubles

We were told that doubles evolved to feed Indian field workers, cheaply and quickly. They offered the flavors of home in a quickly prepared hand food. Today, doubles are served in the early morning from carts on street corners. They are assembled to order in a deft show of flying hands and spoons. A flat disk of fried bread, yellow with turmeric, is retrieved from a warmer. The vendor swipes on a mash of curried chick peas, usually with dhal (yellow split peas). A dollop of one or more chutneys (mango, coconut, tamarind, and more) are added, followed by hot pepper sauce to order. "Slight" is the local term for easy on the hot peppers. From there it goes to volcanic.

The assembly is topped with a second bread disk (hence the name) and then folded and wrapped in paper. It is a wonderful meld of textures, flavors, and spices. We couldn't get enough of them and our first order of business on any trip was a stop at the local doubles vendor.

Roti

A Roti is a wrap of curried vegetables and meats. The wrap is a flat wheat bread. The meat can be chicken, beef, goat, or fish – whatever is available. The bread is filled with meat and sauce and then tucked and rolled, like a Mexican burrito. Optionally, you can order it "bussup" which means to serve the bread on the side.

The quality and flavor vary widely. Locals seem to like some bone to gnaw on, so you have to be careful. A good roti is full of flavor, spicy, and the bread is delicious. A bad roti (to us) means spitting out bone chunks and endlessly chewing stiff grizzle. Thankfully there are more good than bad.

Callaloo Soup

Callaloo are the leaves of the taro plant, the root of which provides a potato-like staple around the world in tropical climates. Callaloo leaves are cooked like spinach and served as a side dish, usually flavored with garlic. Callaloo soup is Trinidad soul food.

It is usually home prepared and therefore difficult to find in restaurants. Besides the callaloo leaves it includes okra and starts with a good stock, usually chicken. Some cooks add beef or seafood. The soup is flavored with onions, garlic, hot pepper sauce, coconut milk, lime juice, and spices. It is often pureed into a thick green mush. It is incredibly delicious.

Bake and Shark

Jim's friend Ron flew in from New Jersey for a visit. It seemed a good time to try Trinidad's famous "Bake and Shark" at Maracas Beach on the north coast. We arranged for a car and driver from

Jesse's Member's Club service. Matthew arrived early and we headed for the mountains. Mathew was a tall lanky Trini, with a sunny nature and a good sense of humor. He splayed across the driver's seat of his small car looking uncomfortably stuffed.

Our first stop was at Arima for doubles. This was Ron's first introduction to this delicious breakfast food. The vendor had regular doubles and a batter-fried callaloo leaf version. We slurped and slopped and licked fingers, trying out both varieties and praising Matthew's choice.

The road to Maracas Beach winds up into the mountains of Trinidad's northern coast. The views of lush valleys and rain forests were spectacular. High up in the mountains we stopped at the Asa Wright nature center.

Once a cacao plantation, Asa Wright is built on a mountainside among large stands of rainforest. It is famous for the variety of wild birds nearby, and for their hiking trails. There are guided tours in the mornings and afternoons, or you can take a leisurely stroll on your own schedule. The original plantation home has been converted into a visitor's lodge with overnight rooms for rent. It sits atop a hill overlooking a wide valley. Overnight visitors enjoy dinner with a view of the valley and mountains beyond while hummingbirds sip at nectar-filled pots by the windows.

We took a guided trail walk and saw a number of hummingbirds, nests of leaf-cutter ants, rare non-nocturnal bats, and a variety of flowers, herbs, and fruit trees. The air was cool and moist and the sky was deep blue; the view over the fields to the mountains was spectacular. We envied those staying overnight, enjoying the cool air and hiking the longer and more interesting trails.

We resumed our drive up and crossed to the ocean side. We descended down and ran along the coastal road. It curves around one beautiful bay after another, with crashing surf and steep cliffs that lead up high hills overlooking the sea. The most picturesque of the bays was Maracas Bay, a sweeping arc of white sand lined with palm trees.

The real treat at Maracas, however, was the best fish sandwich we ever ate. Matthew parked and we headed without delay to the vendor shacks that line the road. Matthew directed us to his favorite. Tables were set outside under umbrellas next to a small building. Inside the building was a serving counter, and next to it a large table under a tent with over twenty condiments and sauces.

I stepped up to the counter and ordered my sandwich. After taking my money the cook grabbed a "bake" which is a bun of fried bread. He split the bread with a large knife and then plopped a piece of freshly fried baby mako shark on it. I then carried my plate over to the condiment table. The proper etiquette is to slop on as much as possible. I did my best, taking spoonfuls of hot red sauce, green herb sauce, garlic sauce, honey/mustard dressing, and then adding cucumbers, cabbage, tomatoes, and a piece of pineapple. I carried the bulging sandwich to one of the outdoor tables with a wonderful view of the palm-lined beach.

The combination of ingredients sounds awful, but it was incredibly delicious. Without a doubt it was the best fish sandwich any of us ever tasted. The fish was wonderfully fresh and sweet and the bun was delicious. There was no taste of grease. The toppings miraculously enhanced each other, rather than clashed. I returned for a second sandwich, which I devoured only a little slower than the first. Ron and Mathew split a another sandwich.

After lunch we waded out into the ocean, beyond the breakers, and played toss with a small coconut. The water was warm and clear and only waist high; the bottom was pure white sand. The waves that rolled past us broke long and slow. After an hour of floating and playing coconut we body-surfed the waves. It was a perfect day at the beach.

MAYORA

(first published in the Caribbean Compass Magazine
www.caribbeancompass.com)

Standing on a sidewalk in Port of Spain we feasted on doubles, the local breakfast of fried flat bread, split and filled with curried chickpeas and spices. We were headed to Trinidad's Atlantic Coast on a three-day photography expedition with Roger, a fellow cruiser and semi-pro photographer, and another couple. None of us knew what to expect; even our Member's Club driver Marlon was not familiar with the area. Anxious and excited, we washed our hands in the jug water at the curb and climbed into the van.

We took the Eastern Main Road, which crosses Trinidad along the forest-covered northern mountains, through Arima and Valencia to Sangre Grande. The terrain varied from hills, to flat farms, to thick jungles of twisted trees. We passed a hitchhiker, slinging a machete at his side. There were brown and white cattle grazing under signs for the "Deliverance Temple," and "City Limitz: free drinks every Friday night." After the crowded streets of Sangre Grande, the road climbs up into the mountains. Our van careened around curves cut into the steep cliffs, lush with the vibrant greens of tropical vegetation. Cresting the last hill, we caught our first view of the Atlantic Ocean.

We descended to coconut tree-lined Manzanilla beach where we stopped to stretch our legs. At the water's edge the trees bend in gentle arcs to the sun. We came upon a mound of discarded coconut shells, ten feet high and more than 30 feet long. A hawk landed in the trees and then flew off to circle majestically overhead. Atlantic waves, muddy with river run-off, lapped the shore. We were to find this same brown water all along the coast; it discouraged swimming, but it did not detract from the beauty.

We continued south on the coastal road, past a long breakwater being built to keep away the sea. As we approached Mayora, Marlon had to call for directions to locate the house we had rented. We walked through the house and flipped coins for the best rooms.

After a quick lunch at a local cafe we returned north to Radix Point, a high-hilled peninsula jutting out into the ocean. The road to the point quickly narrowed to a dirt path. As it gained altitude it wound like a snake and degraded into ruts and rocks. The road challenged Marlon's skills, and repeatedly tested the bottom structure of the van.

There was a vacation house at the top of the hill. After gaining permission from the current renters, we climbed down a path that descended through the forest to the sea. It ended atop a cliff over the beach where a rope, tied to a tree, dangled off the side. One at a time, we grabbed the rope and slid down the face of the cliff. The rocky shoreline was deserted. We took off our shoes and explored, and sat dreaming on the rocks. It was lovely and we left reluctantly, climbing back up the hill to our van. We drove to a local church to photograph.

That evening we met in the living room for cocktails. Roger downloaded our cameras to a laptop and created a common folder of our best pictures. We were determined to learn from him to improve our photography. The digital revolution made this process fun and easy.

Later, our hostess (and house manager) served a dinner of Callaloo soup, marinated chicken, and a macaroni and cheese pie, with plenty of hot sauce. Her cooking was an unexpected treat.

The next morning the alarm sounded at 5 a.m., and we reluctantly rolled out of bed. After a quick cup of coffee, we drove to a nearby beach. The angular dawn light revealed appealing forms and contrasts, especially where a creek clashed with the incoming ocean currents. The sky filled with billowing clouds, backlit by the rising sun. A magnificent squall built to the northeast. There was a pirogue anchored on the beach. We got some of our best pictures that morning, and thoroughly enjoyed the beach walk.

We returned to a breakfast of salt fish, avocado, and coconut bread. After several helpings we turned on the TV to witness the aftermath of hurricane Katrina, which had left a swath of destruction along the gulf coast from New Orleans to Mississippi.

That afternoon we drove south to Galeota Point, stopping at several places to photograph. We discovered that Galeota Point itself is off-limits, the private reserve of petroleum companies. We asked permission to walk the beach at the Coast Guard station and were chased off with a sub-machine gun.

We continued west around the southern corner of Trinidad, observing some interesting signs: "Slow Humps Ahead" (thankfully, we missed the fast ones), "Back in Times" (Returning when?), and our favorite, a building labeled "Fiscalizing Facility."

Lunch was curried duck with local side dishes at the "Sea Wall Bar." Marlon painted his hand, missing the "Wet Paint" signs. Fortunately there was a jug of turpentine handy. Afterwards, we returned to Mayora for rum and beer. Our photo-evaluation cocktail hour had become a serious matter.

A pattern emerged in our photography. Although we each photographed the same scene and in many cases the identical subject, our pictures were significantly different. There was always one that stood out. It had a unique angle, a clearer composition, and better lighting. With Roger coaching we learned from each other.

Dinner that night was stewed kingfish served with a vegetable rice and coleslaw.

The alarm chirped cheerfully at 4 a.m. the morning of our third and final day. We dragged ourselves up and packed. We had arranged for a boat and a guide to take us into the Nariva Swamp. When we arrived it was pitch black, the only sound the rustling of land crabs trapped in nearby barrels. Our guide arrived after dawn and we piled into his boat to head into the swamp.

The channel wound through bushes and grasses to "Bush-Bush" Island. Flocks of ducks flapped over the water and hawks soared overhead. A heron stood in the shallows. Ashore, we spotted red howler monkeys high in the trees. We saw two more groups of monkeys as we walked the path around the island.

There were wildly shaped trees, vines and bromeliads, flowering bushes, huge sculpted leaves, and intricate spider webs. Sunlight filtered through the canopy making the leaves glisten like stars. A Toucan, perched atop a dead tree, lowered his majestic beak and eyed us curiously; he cocked his head and then flew away into the cover of the forest. We almost tripped over a green parrot snake, interrupting it mid-meal, a frog half swallowed in its mouth.

When we returned to the boatman's house the dogs were playing and the blue crabs were clacking their claws aggressively. We ate an early lunch in town and then photographed a bison grazing among the coconut trees.

Reluctantly, we headed back to Chaguaramas.

PORT OF SPAIN

Emil and Olena moved off *Unicorn* to condo-sit for friends in a relatively upscale section of Port of Spain. One Saturday we hopped a maxi-taxi to visit.

Port of Spain is the capital of the republic of Trinidad and Tobago. It lies on the northwest coast, about an hour's ride from Chaguaramas. It is the retail, financial, and government center of Trinidad, and a busy commercial port. Port of Spain offers the benefits and the risks of any large city. The streets are busy with shops, but there are sections to avoid for fear of robbery, or worse.

We hiked across town from the taxi depot to the condo. Olena served lunch, and we discussed the latest world events. They then led us on a walk across town stopping at their favorite stores. The town is well-known for fabric retailers and the variety and prices were amazing.

That afternoon we strolled around Queen's Park Savannah. The park acts as a buffer between the downtown area and the surrounding foothills. It has walking paths, soccer fields, and gardens. Along the drive that circles it are the "magnificent seven."

These seven large mansions were built by the "chocolate barons" in the early 1900's, each trying to outdo the other. Modeled after

European castles and palaces (two have large clock towers), they stand as relics of ostentatious wealth. One is now a college, and several house government agencies. It was a lovely afternoon walk, admiring the architecture, the park, and the view of the hills. We stopped at a street vendor displaying piles of coconuts in the bed of a pickup truck. To order, he lopped off the top of an iced coconut with a machete and poured its water into a plastic cup.

During our stay in Trinidad, there were several kidnappings for ransom each week, and about once a month somebody set off a bomb in a trash can in Port of Spain. It was not the most stable republic in the world.

CENTRAL MARKET

Jesse dropped us off one Saturday morning in Port of Spain at the entrance of the central market. It was loud and frantic; the street was crowded with people coming and going on foot and from a steady flow of cars and vans. We walked through the entrance doors of the large, steel-roofed building. The first room was an open food court set with tables; vendor booths lined the walls. Among the treats sold were curried stews, cow heel soup, and rotis. Across the room through a second set of doors was the fish and meat market.

The fish and meat market was a long rectangular room with high open windows. Stalls were arranged in rows along the walls and down the middle, leaving an aisle on each side. Fishes were on the left and meats on the right. Each stall was set up with tables, knives, and saws; the sides were tiled and there were sinks with running water.

The fish sellers scaled, slit, and gutted fish of varying sizes, shapes, and colors, stacked next to their cutting boards. There were also piles of shrimp and baby sharks staring confused and open toothed. In one stall a vendor sliced steaks off a large tuna hung on a hook. Across the aisle sides of beef, gutted pigs, and cut up goats were strung up or laying on tables. A pile of chickens lay next to a stack of plastic bags.

We walked down the aisle taking in the sights and smells and at the opposite end emerged outside into the open-air market. Several acres of land were filled with tables, roofed booths, and pickup trucks, all overflowing with fruits, vegetables, herbs, plants, and flowers. There were narrow paths which wound through the vendors. It was crowded and noisy, filled with life, colors, and smells.

The variety of produce was mind boggling and the quality was wonderful. Most was freshly harvested that morning or the previous afternoon. Nothing was wilted or old. The vendors were friendly and helpful. Many were farmers and others simply entrepreneurs working a mark up. There were Rastafarians, old people, youngsters, and whole families. We talked and sniffed and bought as we strolled, filling our arms with bags.

There were several varieties of melons, yellow and cream colored gourds and squashes, carrots, dasheen, and cassava; there were baghi (spinach), callaloo, lettuce, chives, and bok choi; there were red tomatoes, green cucumbers, and red, yellow, and green sweet and hot peppers; there were avocados, purple eggplants, yellow papaya as big as footballs, mangoes, cabbages, garlic, onions, and chayottes; there were bananas and plantains, yellow ripe, brown aged, and green; there were green beans a foot and a half long wrapped in bundles, and six inch long okra piled on tables; there were live blue land crabs in buckets, and truck pickup beds filled with brown coconuts; there were parsley, thyme, rosemary and other fresh herbs; there were limes and sour oranges; there were tables stacked with fragrant spices, cinnamon bark, and bottled sauces, green, red and yellow; there were flours, oils, and canned Indian products; there were ginger root, and bundles of sugar cane stalks; there were fresh eggs; there were orange, yellow and red flowers, and green plants. And finally, at the back of the market was a doubles vendor. We would start there on our next visit.

Our senses exhausted, we returned to the fish market and picked out a yellow tail snapper. We then caught up with our cruising friends in the food court. Jesse pulled up in his van and we piled in with our produce for the return ride to Chaguaramas.

We returned often to stock our galley, always amazed.

THE POTTERY FACTORY AND TEMPLES

Early one October morning we and Roger, our photographer friend from the Mayora trip, loaded into Mathew's car to head south.

"Doubles then," Mathew said. We quickly assented. "I know just the one," he added. Everybody seemed to have a favorite doubles vendor. Unfortunately Mathew's was south of Port of Spain, keeping us hungry for another hour. As we approached the town Mathew called the vendor on his cell phone.

"No doubles," he frowned.

"What?" We were incredulous.

"Too late," Mathew shrugged. He pulled over at the vendor's cart. What was left were aloopies, a kind of spicy potato pie. They were not doubles, but they were delicious. Our hunger sated, we climbed back into the car and headed for Ajoupa.

The road wound up into hills of grazing pastures and farms, reminiscent of English countryside. At the top of a high hill we turned into a driveway and parked near a comely white and rose two story home. The home was designed and built by artists Rory and Bunty O'Conner. It was a uniquely open architecture with wide windows, an outdoor staircase, and large French doors leading to porches and balconies. Their property covers the hilltop overlooking a beautiful valley and distant mountains. The yards were landscaped with trimmed gardens, local plants, and flowering trees.

Bunty led us on the short walk from the house to their workshop, a large framed out-building. Piles of clay were heaped next to the building. She and Rory had traveled the country trying various clays before settling on their sources. They used a brick clay mixed with gravel mining waste from nearby Matura. The dry clay was turned with water in a large cement mixer, and then the mud was sieved into a large vat. When it dried to the proper texture it was formed into rectangular slabs. Inside the workshop these slabs were cut up in chunks for sculpting and rolled into sheets.

Bunty specializes in mosaics. She sketches a drawing on a large piece of paper. It might be a floral arrangement, turtles swimming, a landscape, or anything else that strikes her imagination. She cuts off a piece of the sheet clay and traces the drawing onto it. Then she cuts the clay along the lines with a razor knife. The pieces are separated, painted in brightly colored glazes, and baked. They are reassembled with grout and the final piece is baked again. The result is a mosaic similar to stained glass.

Rory creates sculptures from free clay and forms vases on a potter's wheel. The vases are colorfully attractive and the sculptures are imaginative. We noticed a few works in progress: a woman with a basket on her head, a couple about to kiss, and a large iguana.

The workshop has a reputation for small houses. These are crafted by local artists from clay sheets. They first assemble sides and a roof, which are trimmed decoratively. Windows and a door are cut out, a porch is added, and then people and chairs. It is painted in bright Caribbean colors and then baked. Each house is a unique work of art.

Matthew took us to a large grocery store which served a lunch buffet on the second floor. The foods were freshly made. We especially enjoyed the curried mashed pumpkin and the bhagie, sautéed spinach with lots of garlic. After lunch we drove to the small seaside town of Waterloo, to visit the Hindu "Temple of the Sea."

We parked on a causeway leading to a small island where the temple sits out in the Gulf of Paria. It was built by one man over many years. After working the fields all day he carried dirt in the dark, one bucket at a time, to build the causeway and island. Then, he constructed the temple. This was all because the sugar and cocoa barons of the day would not permit any temples on land.

The temple was a large circular room with windows overlooking the sea. The room was dominated by brightly colored statues. These were larger than life representations of the Hindu deities, Lord Ganesh, Lord Hanuman, Mother Durga, Lord Krishna, and Lord Shiva. They were works of art fit for a museum. We were saddened to learn that not long after our visit the temple was vandalized and the statues were broken up.

On the beach were large concrete slabs used for cremations. We witnessed a ceremony in progress, a huge bonfire of logs with a body laid on top. There was a crowd of relatives and friends watching and waiting. When the head explodes in a loud bang the dead person's spirit is thought to leave and rise to the hereafter. We did not wait for the bang.

We drove next to the Karya Siddhi Hanuman Temple. Near the temple was an 85 foot tall Lord Hanuman. The rose-colored temple itself was huge, about the size of a football field and maybe forty feet high. Replicas of what appeared to be other temples were carved in the roof. It was hand sculpted by over 200 artists imported from India. Their intricate works were carved into the roof, around windows, on columns, and in the ceiling.

PITCH LAKE

One sunny morning a group of ten cruisers loaded into Jesse's van for a trip to La Brea. Our first priority was, of course, doubles. We enjoyed several, along with sahina, which is callaloo and split peas wrapped in a fried dough.

La Brea (Spanish for "tar") is a small town in southwestern Trinidad, named for the nearby Pitch Lake. This is where the earth decided to bubble up hot asphalt. The gooey, black, steamy stuff was originally discovered by Sir Walter Raleigh and used to caulk his ship. Since then it has been mined and shipped around the world primarily for road construction.

The lake occupies about 100 acres and is a few hundred feet deep. It is one of only a few known asphalt sources in the world. Another is the famous La Brea Tar Pits in California where the remnants of dinosaurs were found. Trinidad's Pitch Lake is the only lake currently mined, making it the world's only source of natural asphalt.

Over the last 100 years, 15 million tons of asphalt have been removed from the lake. This has caused its surface to drop 70 feet and the surrounding land to cave and buckle. The streets and sidewalks of La Brea are broken and up-heaved, and the houses are tilted and warped.

The lake itself is water and asphalt in three stages. The hot liquid which seeps up from the depths is called the "mother." Exposed to air and cooler temperatures it eventually gels into the "soft" stage, which is the goo that is mined. Left alone soft asphalt eventually stiffens into a semi-rigid surface called "hard." You can walk on the hard and the miners drive bulldozers and other equipment over it. Just don't stand in one place too long. After only a few minutes your footprints are half an inch deep. If you don't move you would share an unpleasant experience with the dinosaurs of California.

After a speech in the small visitors center a guide led us out onto the lake. She carefully followed known paths of hard asphalt, stopping near pools of mother which she scooped up with a stick to demonstrate its liquidity. This was an odd experience, walking by pools of steaming asphalt on an unmarked path.

We were constantly warned to follow our guides footsteps. It didn't take much convincing.

RETURNING NORTH

Our final few weeks in Trinidad began with a quiet dinner aboard to celebrate our 17th wedding anniversary. The next day we began preparations for our journey back north to Florida.

    First on the agenda was the engine. After changing the oil, I tested the alternator pulley repair and tuned the alignment. It performed flawlessly. However, the engine overheated. It seemed our mechanic had left some air inside the water cooler. The engine burped, revealing a low level of coolant. I topped it up and the problem was solved.

    We had a welder fashion a mast pulpit. I drilled holes through the deck on either side of the mast. I then filled the holes with epoxy, and when hardened, drilled a smaller hole in the epoxy. This would keep water from seeping into the wood of the deck. I bolted the pulpit to inside backing plates, using copious gobs of marine adhesive as further insurance against water intrusion.

    We had a carpenter split our engine enclosure into three pieces which latch together. This made it quick and easy to check and service the engine. Previously we had to lift the entire box in one piece, swivel, and set it on the salon floor. This was an awkward task, especially underway. Now we could simply unlatch the top and leave the sides in place. It was Karin's idea and it worked extremely well.

We had some people chores too. A dentist crowned my St. Thomas root canal, and Karin caught a bad sinus infection, which she healed with some super-antibiotics.

More chores for Jim: up the mast to grease the halyard sheaves and down into the hull to tighten up the steering cables; clean out the head hoses; sew repairs in the sails; and secure spare water and fuel containers on deck. More chores for Karin: maxi-taxi runs to grocery stores to stock up our depleted supplies; scrub and polish the topsides; inspect, repair, and fold up the awnings; wrap up the laundry.

After our brush with Emily we had been safe and sound in Trinidad, while north the world had been ravaged by hurricanes. It had been the worst season on record. The last storm was named Beta because they ran out of reserved names. At the end of October with the weather finally showing signs of settling, there was a low rumble one night. It was a 5.5 Richter earthquake off the north coast of Trinidad. We waited for a tsunami which thankfully didn't develop. We hoped this was nature's punctuation mark, a period not a comma, to mark the end of hurricane season.

Tuesday November 8, with the help of six fellow cruisers to shuffle boats and handle lines, we pulled *Nalani* off the Tropical Marine docks. After clearing the moorings we engaged gear. *Nalani* began to make way, vindicating our bottom cleaner's plastic bag theory. We docked at Customs to clear out, and then headed into Chaguaramas harbor.

Half-way across the harbor a squall hit. Blinded by thick rain we turned *Nalani* into the strong wind and slowed to idle speed. A steep swell quickly built and tossed us side to side. We followed the wind shifts, hoping to not run into anything. After about ten tense minutes the squall moved on, and the wind and seas subsided. We noted our position and resumed our departure.

We entered the Boca de Monos and then turned into Scotland Bay to anchor overnight. The bay is on the Chaguaramas peninsula, but it is an entirely different world. It is wild jungle with no roads connecting it to civilization. We were surrounded by steep green hills, home to red howler monkeys and parrots. We watched a hawk soar on the breeze and a sea turtle swim by our hull. The water was clean and clear and there was a cool fresh breeze.

It smelled of renewal.

Part Five

Nutmeg Breeze

Sitting on deck at the bow
After dinner, rum, blues, and love
Quiet, calm, and black
Unfamiliar stars overhead
Orion lying on his side coming over the western hill
Mangroves and hills surround us
Joy swells up inside me

A sudden recognition of how wonderful life is
Here, now, in this place, at this time.
My thoughts scatter through all the fine times
On the water, at the beaches
It is as if the travels of the last year
Were the purpose of it all

A light cool breeze on bare skin
I try to feel chill but cannot
My skin is only refreshed
The exuberance of my soul seeping out my pores
And my breath
From a flaming fire inside

Me and the black night
And the cool breeze and quiet stars
Have I ever felt better?
I can't remember a time
But I will remember this inexpressible happiness
This night
In a deserted cove
On the southern coast
Of Grenada

PRICKLEY BAY
GRENADA
12° 00' N 61°46' W

We motored across calm Scotland Bay into a churned up Boca de Monos. The outgoing current clashed against the incoming tide, creating sloppy chop and swirling side currents. We rode it like a carnival ride, nudging *Nalani* to the middle of the channel to maintain some control.

After a rollicking ride we flushed out into an ocean of soft swells. The sky was clear blue and there was a slight breeze. We set course north for Grenada. It was an odd feeling. After a year of trekking south at the speed of a fast walk, we were turned around and heading back north.

Our feelings churned like the channel. Tired of bobbing port to port, Karin was happy to be heading to a settled home. I was sad. I would miss the life of a nomad. We both agreed, however, that we looked forward to exploring Grenada, which we had missed on our way south.

It was late afternoon. We had timed our departure to reach Grenada at dawn the next morning. Then, if we had problems, or slowed down for any reason, we still had a good chance to arrive in daylight. We motored until dusk when the wind picked up. We hauled sail and eased north on a nice beam reach. The seas became sloppy and confused as the currents shifted direction and speed. The breeze freshened and then lightened, but it kept us moving. *Nalani* slipped and slid steadily north, under control of the autopilot. We napped in shifts.

At dawn we sighted the hilly coast of southern Grenada. It was speckled with black squalls. We started the engine and dropped the sails. Karin took the helm while I secured the deck. She was so sick she could hardly stand. Something she ate had disagreed with her, or she had caught a virus.

We worried about the lack of visibility in squalls near the shoals around the harbor. As we headed for the entrance to Prickley Bay I kept a close eye on the GPS, and I took frequent manual sights to confirm our position. I wanted to know exactly where we were if we suddenly lost visibility. Karin gamely held the helm forcing herself to stay upright. We found the entrance to the bay and made it inside before any squalls hit.

After we anchored Karin went below to sleep. I reheated some leftover pasta and tossed in a couple of eggs and hot sauce, and then wolfed it down with a beer. I was excited to be at Grenada: nutmeg and revolution, mangoes and Ivan. There was much to see and learn.

An unexpected tropical depression (#27 of the season) formed to the north and brought bands of storms over Grenada. We rolled unmercifully as swells swept unmolested into the anchorage. There were torrential rains, from one squall after another for three days. Charly and Francoise, who had arrived before us, fled to the more protected harbor at St. Georges. When the sun finally broke through the morning of the fourth day we moved to Mount Hartman Bay.

Mount Hartman Bay lies to the immediate east of Prickley Bay, but it is more enclosed and better protected. We had had it with the rocking and rolling. The channel through the fringing reefs into Mt.

Hartman bay is not marked, and it is not straight. If you study the charts and have good visibility, it is not too difficult. We wouldn't try it in other than ideal conditions. Once inside, the bay opens up and is beautiful. It is a only a short walk over a hill to Prickley Bay, but it is a different world.

Prickley Bay is crowded and rolly and ringed by shops, boat yards, and noisy roads; Mt. Hartman Bay is nestled among hills with grazing mules and cows and private homes. The shores are natural mangroves and the only noise is from frogs and birds. There is no shopping and no traffic. There is one small marina which provides the essentials of fuel, garbage disposal, water, and internet/telephone access. To us, it was ideal.

REVOLUTION, CHOCOLATE, AND RUM

One sunny morning we hiked up the hill from Mount Hartman Bay to Inga's house. Inga broadcasts on the local VHF as "Homeward Bound" and provides services and communications to cruisers. She had arranged for an island tour, signing up a party of ten. At her house we met the other eight cruisers and our guide, Cutty. We boarded Cutty's van and descended the hill to the road to St. George's.

St. George's is the capital of Grenada. It was built in an old volcanic depression on the southwest coast. A natural harbor protects it from the sea, and it is surrounded by hills. The streets are narrow and hilly, with red roofed buildings of the close cropped French look. It is too busy to be quaint, and to provincial to be a city; it is an ideal old style Caribbean town.

Up one of the hills, overlooking the town and harbor, are two forts and a prison. One of the two forts was bombed by U.S. forces during the 1983 invasion. Unfortunately, at the time the Grenadian troops were in the other fort; the bombed fort was being used as a mental hospital. This was one of the few mistakes U.S. forces made in successfully seizing control of the island from a Cuban-inspired military coup, which had toppled the already Marxist leaning rule of

Maurice Bishop. Democracy was restored and the Cubans were expelled. There are numerous graffiti messages adorning the roads thanking the United States for restoring freedom to the people. There is an overwhelming attitude of good will towards the United States. Near the forts is a prison where the coup leaders, responsible for killing Bishop and others, were held until Hurricane Ivan freed them. Some were still at large during our visit.

From St. George's Cutty drove inland. The country is hilly farmland between the interior mountains and a rocky coast. The roads are steep, winding, and narrow. Many homes are built into hillsides. The coast is ragged, with small harbors and lovely contours. Damage from Ivan was evident everywhere: fallen trees, roofless homes, broken fences, and many buildings hobbled together with temporary roofs and patched walls. All the nutmeg and most of the fruit trees were gone. The remaining scattered trees offered only a hint of the unique smells and tastes that had once dominated this lush and fruitful land. Cutty thought it would take thirty years to restore its previous glory.

We stopped at Mt. Carmel and hiked along a thin creek to a pretty waterfall. At its foot was a natural pool formed in the rocks. The pool was clean and refreshing. We then drove to Grenville for lunch. Afterwards we toured the Grenada Cooperative Nutmeg Association plant.

The plant was opened for us by a manager who acted as a guide. Ivan had destroyed the island's nutmeg trees, which had been a major export. Prior to Ivan the plant ran two shifts seven days a week. It was now open for only one shift, one day a week. We saw how the husks were shucked and the mace separated from the nut. Mace and nut then dry for weeks, after which the nut is cracked to remove the inner nutmeg. A portion of nutmegs are set aside to make jelly, jam, oil, and soap.

Cutty next took us to a colorful two story home painted in Caribbean greens and blues. Behind the house was a forest of cocoa trees, and in the yard were large solar panels and a diesel generator. This was the Grenada Chocolate Factory.

Each room on the first floor was set aside for one phase of making chocolate. Cocoa pods were fermented and dried outside and then roasted in the first room. When done they were processed by a winnowing machine, which breaks up the pods and separates the meat from the shells. It vibrated them over a series of screens. The meat was then ground, stirred, aerated, and heated, in a process called conching.

Conching removes volatile off-flavors and concentrates the chocolate. The thick, hot sludge was then tempered to solidify it and rolled and molded. Each step had a dedicated-purpose machine. The final products were organic chocolate bars with up to 82% cocoa fat, cocoa butter, powder, and lotions. The entire operation was owned and run by three people with machinery they bought used and refurbished themselves. On sunny days it was all powered by the sun; the generator kicked in on cloudy days.

The fishing village of Sauteurs sits atop a hill overlooking the ocean on the northern coast. We walked though an old courtyard to a path that led uphill to a line of bushes. The path ended at a sheer cliff 120 feet high, overlooking the ocean. Straight down waves broke over large rocks at the water's edge.

After the French settled Grenada they tolerated the local Carib natives for a time. In 1651 they decided to wipe them out. The Caribs fought to a last stand at Sauteurs. Most were killed and the remainder, deciding not to surrender, gathered and formed a line. The line led to the cliff, and one by one they leapt off to certain death. The cliff is called, appropriately, "Caribs Leap." Over 2,000 natives died, but how many were killed by the French and how many leapt is unknown.

The River Antoine Rum distillery was built on the river upstream of Antoine Bay. We watched rum produced by traditional methods from sugar cane. A water wheel, powered by the river, grinds the cane to extract the sugar, which is then cooked with water into a syrup. The fire is fueled by dried leftover cane husks. The syrup is fermented in huge vats and then distilled and filtered into a pure white rum. We tasted their 138 proof rum, in small sips. Because it is illegal to transport spirits that strong on an airplane, they offer a milder 80 proof version. We had the advantage of our own transportation and therefore elected to carry a bottle of the firewater home.

At Pearls airport, which is no longer operational, the rotting hulks of two planes sit on the runway. One was to carry off Cuban soldiers; the other was for the coup leader and his entourage. Both were disabled by American firepower before they could take off. They serve as reminders of the revolution.

In the middle of Grenada is the Grand Etang reserve, a mountainous region with the beautiful Grand Etang lake. Once a thick rain forest, the mountains were a ghost town of trees. From a distance they looked normally green, but up close you saw only the brown skeletons of once lush trees wrapped in opportunistic green vines.

It will take centuries to restore the rainforest from Ivan's wrath.

A GIRL AND A BOY

We were enjoying a lunch of pumpkin soup at a cafe on Grand Anse beach, south of St. George's. Our table was outside facing the sea. A girl came walking up the beach, slowly, with no apparent purpose. She wore a school uniform of a white blouse and a green skirt. She looked fifteen years old and was tall and a bit heavy for her age. She held the remnants of a cigarette picked off the beach. She walked over to our table and asked for a light.

"No, we don't smoke," Karin responded, "and neither should you. It's bad for you."

The girl's eyes narrowed. She studied Karin. Then her features softened and she turned and walked away. A few steps later she looked back at Karin, as if to say something. Then she turned again and hurried up the beach.

We watched her break up the cigarette and empty out the tobacco, dropping the remains in the sand.

I had taken a bus to St. George's for some last minute supplies while Karin stayed aboard to work. Returning, the bus dropped me in the village near Mt. Hartman Bay. As I walked back along the road, carrying my bag of purchases, a young boy, maybe ten or eleven, approached from the opposite direction.

The boy had a tennis ball in his hand. Without warning he threw it at me, on a bounce pass. Reflexively, I shifted my bag to my left arm and reached out my right hand. Surprisingly I caught the ball. I then lobbed it back, as if I did it all the time. He smiled widely.

As we passed, we fist-bumped the play.

CRUISE INTERRUPTED

Our second week in Grenada we received a cryptic email from Karin's parents. They wanted us to call at a specific time to "discuss a matter best on the phone." It was bad news. Karin's father was dying of leukemia and he had six weeks to live.

He had already sold his car and made arrangements, including the posting of a red "Do Not Resuscitate" sticker on the refrigerator. He urged us to keep cruising and having fun, assuming we could hop on a plane at a moment's notice. The reality of cruising is different. If we were still in Trinidad we could have left *Nalani* at the marina. But leaving her alone at anchor for a month or more was simply out of the question. Tropical Storm Gamma had formed off Honduras and the ITCZ was still active.

Karin wanted to see her father while he was still coherent and she wanted to be there for her mother. There was no option but to haul *Nalani* out of the water and fly back to the states.

We took a bus to St. George's with Emil and Olena who had recently arrived at Prickley Bay. We toured the fort, had a nice lunch overlooking the Carenage, and then stopped at a travel agency to buy plane tickets. We would fly Air Jamaica through Kingston to Ft. Lauderdale on December 5 with a tentative return on January 17.

Thanksgiving day we made arrangements to haul out at Spice Island Boat Yard. *Nalani* would be safely blocked up in the guarded yard, and while there they would sand and paint her bottom. That night after a traditional turkey dinner complete with gravy, vegetables and mashed potatoes, we sat on deck under a black sky dazzled by the bright stars.

It was a warm night with a slight breeze and Mt. Hartman Bay was quiet and calm. Our emotions were anything but calm. We worried about leaving *Nalani* alone. She was our home. We feared how we would handle Karin's father dying, while we stood by helpless. We questioned how her mother would react. Could we leave her to return to cruising? When would we be back? Would we have to rush *Nalani* back to Florida in hurried multi-day hops? Or could we take up where we left our cruise? The stars above were disappointingly silent.

The afternoon we hauled *Nalani* we stood by helpless and nervous. Our home was being lifted skyward by a crane. We followed the crane as it crossed the boatyard. What would we do if the crane dropped her? We had no insurance, and we were far from home in a foreign country.

On December 5 we boarded the Air Jamaica flight and left the Caribbean. Leaving *Nalani* behind was difficult. After meeting with the yard personnel we felt confident she would be looked after, but still, she would be alone in the yard. It took a huge leap of faith for us to leave her behind.

In the air flying to Jamaica we began to think of the trip as yet another adventure. We would spend time with Karin's parents while her father was still alive, and provide support to her mother, but we could also visit with other family and friends. We began to feel more like tourists on vacation, trusting *Nalani* would be fine. We enjoyed scoping out the harbors on Jamaica's coast as we glided in for a landing. Our spirits rose further when we landed at Ft. Lauderdale and met my daughter Martine. We would treat this as a sabbatical from cruising.

Christmas Eve we shared dinner with Karin's mother, and her sister and brother-in-law, Donna and Jim. Her father lay drugged in the bedroom under the care of a hospice nurse. Dinner began with a toast.

"To the man of the hour," Karin's mother offered. We ate our meal, feigning normalcy but conscious of her father's waning presence. He passed away that day.

The next few weeks were a blur of activity. Karin's mother began to put her life back together. We alternated between helping her and visiting friends and family. When we finally flew back to Grenada we were saddened by the loss but anxious to return to our adventure.

From the airport we took a taxi to the boatyard. Night had descended and it was densely dark. We punched in our code on the gate lock and it failed to open. After a few more unsuccessful tries we rang the night watchman who admitted us. Our driver helped carry our bags and supplies along the crooked paths between boats to where *Nalani* had been blocked up. The space was empty.

We stood dumbfounded, holding our bags. Our boat was gone and the yard was closed for the night. For a moment I imagined sleeping in the dirt atop our luggage. How could a boat be stolen from the yard? Was this somehow related to our gate code not working? Frightening scenarios raced through our minds. What would we do? Where was our home? It was our worst nightmare and we were living it.

After the initial shock I set off to look for *Nalani*. Karin and our driver stayed with our luggage. Somebody moved the boat, I reasoned. It must still be somewhere in the yard. Nothing else made any sense. I crossed the yard desperate and fearful. Finally I spotted

Nalani blocked up and freshly painted. We later learned that the yard had moved her to make room for another boat. It just didn't seem important to them to tell us.

Overwhelmed by relief, we paid our driver and climbed up the ladder back into our home.

WORKING BOAT RACES

After launching *Nalani* and her freshly painted bottom, we returned to Mt. Hartman Bay to get our sea legs and to prepare for the voyage north. One Saturday we took the day off to return to Grande Anse beach. They were holding working boat races that weekend.

The boats were plywood hulls fat in the beam with bamboo poles for masts. They had gaff-rigged mainsails and jibs. For each trial heat six teams lined up on the beach. At a call they carried their boats into the surf, leaving one member behind. At the start whistle the beached member raced into the surf and jumped into his boat. The remaining crew could then haul themselves aboard while frantically raising sail. All this happened while the surf pushed and turned the boats. Only speed and teamwork got them off.

The boats sailed offshore to a square course which ran down the beach, out to sea, back up the beach, and finally returned to a finish buoy near the surf line. The boats did not go upwind well, and often a losing boat caught just the right angle and sprinted past the pack. It was quite fun to watch. The weather was gorgeous and the sea was an intense blue. A serious all-day party played out on the beach. It was so much fun we decided to return the next day for the finals.

We arrived at high tide. A large crowd overflowed the narrow beach, drinking, smoking pot, and screaming. We walked out knee deep in the sea to find room to watch the junior finals. The surf was huge and one of the boats swamped at the start. The others pushed through the breaking waves into a heavy swell. The swell pulled their bows off the wind, forcing them into unplanned tacks. They flipped and flopped comically, working out to sea. Offshore they sped downwind and then spun around. Without keels the upwind lead changed often, as the boats tacked frantically, trying to minimize their lee drift and gain a competitive angle.

On the final leg two boats finally separated from the pack. They rounded the last buoy and headed towards the beach. Bodies shifted, hanging off the gunnels on gusts, as the boats raced to the finish line. The crowd erupted in chants and screams with everyone jumping and waving. The crews strained to eke out another tenth of a knot.

To a raucous celebration the winning boat careened across the finish line, no more than two feet ahead of the second place boat.

TYRELL BAY
CARRIACOU
12° 27' N 61° 30' W

We sipped wine on deck while the sun descended over Tyrell Bay, Carriacou. We were worn out and sore. It had been a full day of wild and rough sailing north from Grenada.

Our course had taken us directly into twenty knot winds with higher gusts. The seas were choppy in cross currents, and the swell had built to ten feet in places. It was especially rough south of Les Tantes, east of the underwater volcano named "Kick-Em Jenny." Though the volcano, whose top is within 600 feet of the surface, has not erupted since 2001, it still makes a jumbled mess of the seas. We managed only slow progress, tacking back and forth using the engine and tightly trimmed sails.

We had been forced to hand-steer, falling off the steep waves to avoid burying the bow, and then cutting forward in the troughs. Waves constantly broke over the bow sending torrents of blue water down the decks. Buckets of spray crashed against the cockpit window. During the worst of it we had to douse the jib. It was tiresome and nerve wracking.

As we approached Carriacou the wind eased and the seas settled. Our entrance into Tyrell Bay was calm and anticlimactic but a wonderful relief. Our decks and sails were salt-soaked, and we were tussled and worn.

Carriacou is the southern limit of the East Caribbean rental fleet. Vacationers fly in and pick up sailboats from large fleets stationed from St. Vincent to Canouan. These boats cruise the Grenadines and the popular Tobago Cays. A few wander down to Carriacou. Many are experienced boaters, but some are not.

As we nursed our sore muscles and scrapes an obvious rental boat motored into the bay and bellied up next to *Nalani*. The entire bay behind us was open and yet they dropped their anchor no more than six feet off our bow. I walked forward and politely asked them to move, pointing to all the available space. The captain nodded and gestured to his mate on the bow, who pressed the up button on their electric windlass.

They circled around to a position aft of our stern. I signaled thumbs up and the captain yelled to the mate to drop the anchor. The mate hit the wrong button and the anchor went up instead of down, jamming itself in the chocks. This initiated ten minutes of screaming and banging on the anchor by both of them while the boat drifted aimlessly. It was quite the show, amusing only because they were safely behind us.

Night descended and the anchorage quieted. Everyone settled; there would be no more boats. You usually don't navigate near shore after dark in the Eastern Caribbean. You have to read the water, and there are no lights or other navigational aids.

Two boats motored into the bay that night with search lights blazing. The first was reasonably prudent; he dropped his anchor aft of the fleet. The second wove through the anchored boats waving his light left and right, forward and back, as he jostled to head of the harbor.

We licked our wounds in Tyrell Bay for a week, tightening loose nuts, sealing chain plates, cleaning up the decks, and otherwise securing *Nalani* after her all day bash from Grenada. Carriacou was deserted; most of the restaurants were closed and the streets were empty. We bought a five-pound lobster from a local fisherman.

We put the lobster in the sink and wondered what to do. He was too large by half to fit in our largest pot. He sat deceptively still until I reached in to poke him. He flapped his tail violently and I jumped backwards. I executed him with a large kitchen knife between the eyes.

We boiled the tail and enjoyed a delicious and filling dinner.

THE GRENADINES

From Tyrell Bay we sailed to Union Island, the Tobago Cays, Canouan, and finally Bequia where we stayed two weeks. These are the charter boat cruising grounds and we had plenty of company. The weather was good, but the winds were too strong to relax.

The anchorage at Union Island was small, crowded, and deep. After a few unsuccessful tries at anchoring we opted for one of the moorings. The wind blew strong during our visit, and we were grateful not to worry about the anchor dragging.

We bumped into Charly at the local internet cafe, literally. I broke my sunglass frame giving him a welcome hug. We then toured Clifton with he and Francoise. Clifton is a quaint village of mostly bars, restaurants, and souvenir shops, and was bustling with tourists.

In the Tobago Cays we anchored inside Horseshoe reef by James Island. The scenery was truly idyllic: palm trees, white sand beaches, clear blue waters, and reefs teeming with fish. Unfortunately, we couldn't enjoy it. The wind blew hard every day, creating a heavy chop and making dinghy exploration difficult and snorkeling impossible.

In Charles Bay at Canouan the best anchorage spots were filled with charter fleet buoys. Other cruisers had to huddle along the fringes, and roll on the tides. The wind gusted off the nearby hills, going from zero to twenty knots in an instant. We learned to wait for a lull to launch, or haul up, the dinghy.

At the Tamarind Hotel they graciously took a large bag of garbage off our hands. That was the last -- and only -- free service on the island. We enjoyed a nice lunch of grilled fish at an outrageously expensive 170 EC ($68 U.S). All the pay phones on the streets were vandalized, making the hotel's service the only way to communicate with the outside world. It was priced at a hefty 5 EC per minute.

The village was shabby and deserted. The few locals we passed were sour and unfriendly. The houses on the hills were picturesque, but otherwise it was depressing. A charter boat facility and the Tamarind hotel were nestled together like a protected enclave. We were told that northern Canouan was being developed as a gated community for foreigners, at $1.4 million per lot.

We noticed two bags of garbage floating in the harbor. A third bag had been picked up by a local. He gestured obscenely to the harbor, cursing the floating boats.

From Canouan we sailed to Bequia, again into strong headwinds and raised seas. We bashed and crashed our way slowly. About half way to Bequia we spotted a wall of rain to our east. It stretched north to south with no apparent center. We kept our sails up since it didn't appear to have any circulation. That was a mistake.

We were blasted by a steady 40 knots for about five minutes. We reacted by easing the sheets to avoid a knock down. Even so we buried the lee rail three times. I climbed forward on hands and knees and wedged myself inside the bow pulpit. I was alternately dunked in the sea and blasted by wind gusts. Somehow I managed to pull down the jib and tie it up. *Nalani* then rode out the remaining blow stable and secure. After the sky cleared, the normal 15-20 knot winds resumed.

We made Admiralty Bay, Bequia, and anchored off Princess Margret beach. After spending two days and nights rolling around uncomfortably we moved to the inner harbor and picked up a mooring. This was wonderfully calm and convenient to town, but it was expensive.

Bequia blends their local economy and tourism well. The town is clean and colorful. The locals are friendly and engaged in their own industries of boat building, fishing, and the like. It gets crowded when cruise ships offload passengers, but that doesn't last long. There are good supply stores, groceries, and restaurants. We enjoyed our stay. A hike up the hill, on the northwest side of the harbor, rewards you with a spectacular view of the island, harbor, and sea.

At Friendship Bay, a bus ride across the island, we tried a most unusual drink: Bailey's Irish Cream, a bottle of Guinness, two eggs, a banana, and bitters, whizzed up in a blender with ice. It tasted like a coffee milkshake and was surprisingly delicious.

One afternoon we took our dinghy into town, and then walked back along the harbor's edge for some exercise. We watched a 42' Hallberg-Rassi run aground. We were not too far from the action, so we stopped to watch the drama unfold. The boat hailed a local fisherman who looped a line to their bow. He revved up his engine and began to pull. The sailboat slowly wobbled into deeper water. They continued up the harbor until a strong gust blew sideways and the towing boat lost control.

To our horror they had just passed *Nalani*. We watched helpless and terrified as the heavy cruiser drifted down on our home, crashing into her bow. We flagged a nearby small boat to run us out to *Nalani*, praying the hull had not been holed. In a few minutes our home and all our possessions could be underwater.

We scrambled up her sides and ran to the bow to inspect. There was a large scrape across the bow sprit and the bow pulpit was bent. Some caulking along the rub-rail was uprooted. Considering the force of the collision and the weight of the Hallberg-Rassi, the damage was minor. The owners gave us some cash for repairs. After a couple of coats of paint and some fresh caulk, *Nalani* was back to herself again.

An upper level trough formed, bringing several days of heavy winds and rain. We rode it out, taking full advantage of the restaurants and shops of Bequia. We met Sally and the staff at the Caribbean Compass magazine, which had published two stories of mine.

We decided to make an overnight run to St. Lucia, and waited for a weather window. That opportunity came on a Saturday, ten days after our arrival. We should have waited another day for the winds to go more easterly and calm down. However, we were tired of paying for the mooring and we didn't look forward to another Saturday night of music blasting from town. We paid for our impatience in heavy winds, rough seas, and thunderstorms.

We sailed to the lee of St. Vincent, motoring up the coast in calm conditions. When we reached the northern end of the island all hell broke loose. We set a double-reefed main and staysail and engaged the wind vane. The rest of the night we hunkered down in the cockpit with our enclosure zipped tight and the vane at the helm. It was a chore to use the head or sleep; meals were impossible.

Nalani romped along happily, the vane rolling off the gusts and heading up in the lulls. Seas were 6 to 8 feet and the wind was 20 knots and gusty. We were amazed at how well the vane handled the helm. We could not have done as well. Still it was a sleepless, uncomfortable night.

After midnight we fetched the lee of St. Lucia and lost the wind again. We retired the wind vane and started the engine, grateful for the calm ride up the coast.

Dawn revealed a washing machine of churned up seas as the tide crossed against a freshening wind. Squalls came up with locally heavy winds and quickly building seas. We crashed and bashed our way forward through several of these for two hours. Late morning the skies cleared and we made Rodney Bay. We happily dropped the anchor off Pigeon Island.

After a lunch of hard-boiled eggs, dry sausage, cheese, and beer, we retired for a long afternoon nap. We woke up in time for dinner and a bottle of white wine. After a lovely sunset we returned to bed for a long night's sleep, in glorious flat calm.

RODNEY BAY
ST. LUCIA
14° 05' N 60° 58' W

We moved from Pigeon Island to Rodney Bay Marina. Emil and *Unicorn* were there waiting for Olena to return from a business trip to the Balkans. We enjoyed a reunion lunch at Café Ole with his friends Gordon, Cynthia, and Artois.

Gordon and Cynthia were celebrating their anniversary. He was Canadian and she was St. Lucian. They were married here 40 years ago, and had returned to celebrate. Artois was an ex-pat French Canadian. He was a crusty old man with plenty of stories.

Artois once ran a charter catamaran off Soufriere at the foot of the Pitons. One day he picked up an American couple, floating naked out to sea. They were close to drowning. They said that they had been aboard a rented sailboat when local criminals boarded and tossed them overboard. They did not explain their lack of clothes.

Another time Artois was delivering 60 crates of rabbits from Martinique to St. Lucia. The crates were stacked on the deck of his trawler. In rough seas the crates came loose and broke apart. He told a hilarious story of docking at Castries, where his crew and the customs agents spent the day chasing 300 rabbits around the deck.

We stayed five days in the marina, cleaning *Nalani*, waxing the topsides, and completing minor repairs. We visited with Emil and Olena and stocked up groceries. When it came time to leave, we decided to try the beach on the other side of the spit of land that separates the marina from the bay.

Unfortunately, that anchorage is also popular with tourists on jet skies. They flew by *Nalani*, seeing who could get closest, for sport. One guy actually ran his jet sky under our bow sprit; we thought he would be decapitated, he came that close. After a nervous lunch, we hauled up the anchor and returned to Pigeon Island. There, it was quiet and calm.

The next day we took the dinghy to Pigeon Island. We walked up a steep trail to the top of the hill and toured Fort Rodney. The view was spectacular. To the east was the mountainous interior of St. Lucia, to the south were the Pitons, and to the north were black coral reefs and blue ocean.

We found the narrow rocky trail that leads up Signal Tower hill, the highest elevation on the island. The trail was incredibly steep. Half way up Karin could not pull herself over a large rock, due to the steepness of the trail. I grabbed her hand and pulled while she pushed, and she finally made it over. It was a difficult trail.

When we reached the top we found it flat but only about ten yards across. There was a pole stuck in a mound of dirt to mark the top. To the north the hill dropped off in a sheer cliff. The view was magnificent but chilling. Our feet wobbled. One wrong step, or a good gust, and we could fly off into oblivion. It was as scary as it was beautiful.

We stepped and slid down the trail, working to control our descent. On the other side of the hill was a path that led down to the landscaped grounds of the island's orientation center. There we found, of all things, a stone-walled British pub. We happily ordered cold beers.

ST. LUCIA TO SINT MAARTEN

We left Rodney Bay and crossed the channel to Martinique. The winds were a perfect 12 to 15 knots with just enough easting to sail on course. The swells were comfortably well-spaced and small. The sun broke through overcast skies. We sat back, letting the wind vane handle the helm, and thoroughly enjoyed the easy ride.

We passed by the lovely harbor of Grand Anse D'Arlet and then sprinted across the wide mouth of Fort de France harbor on a lively breeze. We then lost our wind to the mountains of Martinique and had to motor to St. Pierre. We explored the coast north of the town, looking for a suitable anchorage, but had to double back and anchor off the town dock. Thankfully it was a calm night with minimal roll.

We left at dawn the next day, and once clear of mountainous Martinique we enjoyed another lively comfortable sail on easy seas. We crossed the channel to Dominica where once again mountains blocked our wind. We motored up the coast and turned into Prince Rupert Bay, two hours before sunset.

What a difference from our first visit! The anchorage was thick with boats, including three cruise ships. We were quickly accosted by two boat boys and two more on surf boards. They took a firm no with a shake of their heads and moved on. There was too much business in the crowded harbor to waste time arguing with us.

The next morning we crossed to Les Saintes on flat seas under clear skies. There was a nice steady breeze, angled perfectly for a close reach. This was a wonderful sail, moving steady on flat seas at five knots, the wind vane at the helm. We spotted several whales.

We anchored off Le Bourg in precisely the same location as our first visit, off the stern of the very same motor yacht. We rowed into town, cleared customs, and quickly indulged in the creamy chocolate gelato. We purchased a bottle of Guadeloupe Rhum Agricole and some wine. It was good to be back in France.

The winds howled the next few days and the harbor whipped up to a frenzy. Thunderstorms were frequent. A nasty roll worked its way inside, making life aboard miserable. The forecast deteriorated. A ten foot northwest swell was expected to build and roll unmolested into the harbor. We studied the charts and discovered a small anchorage, nicely protected from the northwest, on Terre-de-Bas, called Anse Fielding.

We moved to Anse Fielding the next morning and nestled as high up the cove as the depth would allow. There were no other boats and it was wonderfully calm. Later that day two sailboats arrived and the weather turned ugly. There were frequent thunderstorms with heavy downpours and gusty winds. We rode it out nicely in the protected anchorage.

The next day we waited while the blow wore itself out. The following day we weighed anchor and crossed the channel to Guadeloupe. The wind was slightly abaft of our beam and a strong 20 knots; the seas were a good 8 to 10 feet. This made for a lively rolling reach under double-reefed main and staysail, hand steering to maintain control in the churned up seas. Once in the lee of Guadeloupe the seas flattened, but the breeze kept up. We clocked 8.5 knots at one point, a personal best for *Nalani*.

As we moved up the coast the winds fluctuated between fierce and none, based on the contours of the mountains. It kept us busy with sail changes and intermittent engine power. We finally reached Deshaies at the north end of the island mid-afternoon, thankful to anchor in the calm harbor.

It was gusty the next morning and we decided to lay over, to let the weather settle. We walked around the quaint French town, had lunch and bought some groceries. We were turned away from the local internet cafe because the police were using it. They had no service in their own office. Our lunch was Boudin du Pecheur (a spicy seafood sausage) and grilled red snapper, served with rice and beans, squash, and plantains. We chased it down with a chilled bottle of Grenache rose.

Nobody seemed to work too hard in Deshaies, but they got by nicely. It had a friendly and safe feeling with all the accoutrements of a French village: rustic and colorful architecture, a boulangerie (bakery), a charcuterie (butcher), well-stocked groceries, and plenty of small, family restaurants. It was quiet and reserved, nestled in a bowl of the mountains, disconnected from the mainland as if an island itself. Everybody was very friendly.

The next day we sailed to the volcanic island of Montserrat, with its mounds of ash and rivers of lava. A new settlement clung to the cliffs at the northern end, maintaining an unlikely human presence on the bubbling, spewing, inhospitable land. We kept going and made Nevis near sunset. There was enough light to avoid the many fish traps around the southern end to Charlestown. We anchored off the beach.

We laid over a day at Charlestown, clearing in and out at the same time, accessing the internet and enjoying a lunch of chicken roti. That night I prepared a dinner of canned turkey with rice and beans. I tossed in a few of the sweet peppers we had bought in Deshaies. Soon we were choking. The peppers had been mislabeled; they were fire hot – probably Scotch Bonnets. I picked out what I could and suffered through my plate; it was tasty, but painful. Karin gave up after one bite.

The next morning we were up at 4 a.m. to weigh anchor in the light of a full moon. We motored on calm seas past the cut between Nevis and St. Kitts, not wanting to venture through it in the dark. The engine quit. There was air in the fuel line. I bled the line at the secondary filter and the engine coughed to life. We continued along the coast of St. Kitts.

At the cut between St. Kitts and Statia we hardened sail and headed to sea, keeping upwind of course. It was a long run to Sint Maarten and we wanted insurance against a wind shift. We averaged 6.7 knots that day, slowly falling off the wind to fetch Sint Maarten by mid-afternoon. It was a romping good sail.

SIMPSON BAY LAGOON
SINT MAARTEN
18° 02' N 63° 06' W

We clunked into reverse, spinning the bow and stalling our motion, holding our position in the group of thirty boats. We were waiting for the bridge to open over the canal connecting Simpson Bay to the Lagoon. The Lagoon is an inland salt water lake and the primary anchorage on Sint Maarten.

    The boats appeared disorganized, but when the bridge was raised a disciplined line quickly formed. Each boat was well aware of its position in the queue. We motored through the bridge fourth in line, and as we emerged into the Lagoon we were toasted and hollered at by friendly revelers at a shore side pub. It was happy hour, and happy hour is taken seriously in the Lagoon.

    We rounded the corner and headed up the main channel along land towards the airport. Perpendicular to the channel, were rows of anchored boats, each row separated by its own sideways channel. We had never seen anything like it; it was an organized parking lot of boats.

We bobbed and weaved among the boats searching out space. We finally anchored east of the airport on the fringes of the no anchor region, which was no longer marked nor observed.

It had been a long journey, but we were finally safe and sound in calm, protected waters. We had arrived at the "cruising Mecca" of the Caribbean. It was a significant goal on our homeward bound run. Here we could regroup, repair, and restock for the long haul back to the Bahamas. That night we slept well on flat water, quiet and dark.

Sint Maarten is the Dutch half, and St. Martin the French half of this popular northern leeward island. Beaches, bays, and lagoons fringe a hilly terrain, laced by modern roads and speckled by towns hosting the best shopping in the Caribbean. It is a popular cruise ship destination with over 250 restaurants, more than 700 shops, casinos, and several major European shopping chains. For cruisers Budget Marine and Island Water World, the two biggest chandleries in the Caribbean, are based here.

The most popular anchorage is Simpson Bay Lagoon on the west side of the island. The Lagoon is completely enclosed by land. The only waterway egresses are the canal to Simpson Bay at the southwest corner, and a dredged channel north to Marigot Bay. The northern half lies in French territory and is mostly quiet and remote. The southern half is Dutch, where most boats anchor and shops, marinas and services fringe the shores. The Lagoon is an anchor friendly six to twenty feet deep with good holding. There are only a few small shoals to avoid. It is about a mile wide and three miles long.

Marigot Bay on the French side is also a popular anchorage, and it hosts a large marina. However, it is exposed to the north and not always comfortable. Philipsburg Bay at the capital serves the cruise ships. There are a few other mostly daytime anchorages around the island, subject to conditions.

Sint Maarten is the northern terminus of an annual migration of cruising boats from Grenada and Trinidad. They ride out the blustery winter fronts in the Lagoon and then island hop south in the spring, settling below the hurricane belt for summer. In late Fall they return north. A number of boats are permanent residents and there are frequent temporary visitors. It is an eclectic community of boaters and an ideal place to restock and repair. It is comfortably flat in the protected anchorage and you are surrounded by services, goods, transportation, and modern communication. The U.S. dollar is happily accepted and English universally spoken on the Dutch side. The French side, bubbling over with culture, lip-licking cuisine, and fragrant wine, is only a short dinghy ride north.

Our first day in the Lagoon we launched the dinghy to explore the strip of land that connects the bridge with the airport. We tied up at a marina and walked out to the road. Traffic was backed up by the open bridge. We gaped at the marinas, bars, restaurants, and shops that lined the road; we had become unaccustomed to such commercial denseness. We replenished our funds at an ATM and caught up on our email at an internet cafe. At the bridge we followed the signs to customs where they cleared us in quickly with no fuss.

We walked back to Rics, an American style bar and restaurant that looks out over the lagoon. To our delight, they offered Heineken on tap -- and it was the cheapest beer. We savored large American-style hamburgers with fries, and several drafts. This was civilization.

We returned to *Nalani* for a nap and afterwards took the dinghy to Shrimpies. The ample dock space was crowded. Shrimpies is a gathering place for cruisers offering cheap drinks, good food, laundry service, and fresh water refill at a dollar per jug. It has a decidedly relaxed atmosphere, and offers free electrical outlets and Wi-Fi internet service for laptops. You are welcome to stay as long as you like with no pressure to buy anything.

The next morning was Sunday and we returned to Shrimpies for the weekly flea market. Tables were set up on the dock for cruisers to rent. There were piles of old gear, unwanted supplies, and homemade art works for sale. Shrimpies kicked in a keg of free beer, which helped to draw a crowd. We walked around the tables and bumped into several people we had met in other ports. The flea market is as much a social event as a place to buy and sell.

That afternoon we explored the Lagoon, tying our dinghy up at a number of docks to survey the area. It had a decidedly American feel, something like a cross between Dallas and strip-mall Florida. A few high-end boutiques were sprinkled in for flavor. We were impressed by the number and variety of shops and restaurants. For boaters, there was an Island Water World and a Budget Marine, stocked with anything you needed. At Simpson Bay Marina we discovered Zee Best, a wonderful French bistro where we were to eat a number of meals during our stay.

The harbor itself was mostly quiet, except for the planes that flew low over the water to and from the airport, and the small boats that whiz around careless of noise and wake. At night it was calm and quiet.

Marigot is delightfully French. We enjoyed lunches at Le Longeoir on the waterfront, one of which we shared with Emil and Olena. We had goat cheese over eggplant, seared tuna, scallops and shrimp in an herb-cream sauce, salads and baguettes, and of course, numerous glasses of wine. The waterfront is beautiful with a modern marina, boats at anchor, and a large open-air market of clothes and fabrics. The streets are filled with shops and restaurants, eyeglass stores, boutiques, hardware stores, cafes, and bars.

On the Dutch side we restocked. We found Grande Marche and Cost U Less located across the street from each other on the road to Philipsburg. The former is a huge grocery market, larger than most in the U.S., and the later is a Sam's Club-like warehouse store. We replenished our canned goods and staples like paper towels and toilet paper. We made numerous bus trips over several days, as we could only carry so much back at one time.

We bought several cases of wine, and one of rum, for the bilge. We couldn't ignore the cheap prices. We filled our propane tanks and topped up the fresh water tanks. We took on diesel and gasoline, one jug at a time, running the dinghy back and forth. We serviced the engine and the outboard, repaired rigging, built new anchor snubber lines, and fashioned a jib haul down block and tackle. We began each day with pastries and coffee at a nearby boulangerie. Lunches were usually at a Lebanese restaurant near the canal, at Rics or Shrimpies, and, of course, at Zee Best.

We spent twelve days at Sint Maarten. Along with shopping and work we managed some exploring. We toured the Lagoon and Marigot in our dinghy, indulging in late day beers at the various pubs, often with Emil and Olena. We spent a couple of days hunting for a new shower faucet, finding the perfect one at a hardware store on the Dutch side. Karin was very excited to find it, and we carried it all the way back to the states planning to install it after our cruise (we never did).

During evenings we plotted our return to the states. Emil and Olena decided to take short hops: an overnight to St. Croix, and then to Puerto Rico, the Dominican Republic, and finally the Turks and Caicos. We decided to go to Culebra, and from there make a direct run to South Caicos. It would be the longest single sail we ever undertook, but it would accelerate the voyage home. We thought that after a day or two it would not be any less comfortable than overnight in a rolly anchorage.

So we thought, anyway.

Part Six

Squalls and Rainbows

The sail vane tugs the wheel, pulling Nalani off the wind. We are running west on a broad reach. It's blowing twenty knots, and the seas are six to ten feet. Nalani lifts on the crests and dips into the troughs, rolling side to side. We are in the open ocean somewhere north of the Dominican Republic and south of the Navidad Banks.

Swells slap the hull, tossing froth in the air. We are in the cockpit. Karin is curled up with a jacket sleeping, wedged into the corner of the seat and bulkhead. She sleeps more from exhaustion than choice. I sit sideways and scan the ocean. We have not seen another boat in days, but we still have to keep a lookout. Below, there is a loud chorus of clanging pots, thumping books, and rattling stores shifting about in the cabinets. Water sloshes and slaps against the hull, the rigging twangs and rings, the sails flap, and the hull creaks and groans. Outside, these sounds are subdued and the air is fresh.

Hungry, I step below, holding handrails as the boat rolls and rocks. I brace myself in the galley and light the burner under a pot of leftover stew. The pot is clamped in place. I stir as it warms, and then carry the pot back to the cockpit. I brace myself sideways on the seat, my back against the hull and my feet against the wheel pulpit.

I rock back and forth and scan the seas while I eat spoonfuls of stew. When I finish I return below, one hand on a rail and the other holding the pot. I clamp the pot back on the stove to clean later and stumble forward. The hull rolls side to side as I walk hand over hand on the overhead rail. In a stable moment I open the head door, lift the lid and drop my pants. I sit and press my feet into the walls for balance. I let only a little water into the head because more would slosh out. I pee quickly and flush.

We live this way for five days and four nights. We see no fish, no birds, and no other boats. There is nothing but sky, clouds, and the rolling ocean.

ENSENADA HONDA
ISLA DE CULEBRA
18° 18' N 65° 18' W

While exploring Sint Maarten we underwent a transition. We began to accept that our journey would end and that we had a new life to get busy building. We stocked up, fixed what had to be fixed, serviced the engines, tuned the rigging, and otherwise prepared for one last run. It was 1,200 miles on a direct line to Florida, and although it would take us two months it seemed only a short stroll away. Our meandering north and west was about to become a sprint home.

After scouring the charts and discussing strategies, we decided on an overnight sail to Culebra, where we would stage a direct run to South Caicos. That run would be four or more days and nights of open ocean sailing, passing by Puerto Rico and the Dominican Republic. It would cut a couple of weeks off the more traditional routes. It would also be exhausting and uncomfortable, but we had no idea how much.

The morning of April 1 a whiff of a breeze came up on Simpson Bay Lagoon. There was a refreshing coolness to it, a hint of change like the smell of autumn after a hot summer.

We weighed anchor to make the morning bridge opening and joined a line of five boats, including a 100+ foot mega-yacht. We motored through the open bridge and into Simpson Bay. There was a light breeze and we set full sail, easing off at four knots on a close reach. The sky was a bright blue, painted with strokes of white clouds. The sea was calm. We leaned back and enjoyed a picture perfect start to our run home.

An hour later we lost the wind and had to run the engine. We set the autopilot for Culebra and settled in for a long ride. We motored all that afternoon and early evening, marking our progress with crosses on the chart. We got no push from the anticipated prevailing current.

Later that night the seas built on our beam and we began to roll uncomfortably. Cans and pots banged around in the cabinets. On deck the water jugs worked their ties loose. The anchor clattered and shifted in its chock. We needed handholds to walk even a few steps.

Sometime after midnight a breeze came up; I crawled forward to set the staysail to steady the boat. As soon as the sail was up the wind freshened. We set the engine in neutral and I began to untie the mainsail. We had one spreader light out and the other was half-gone. I cursed myself for not checking these lights in the Lagoon. Before I could haul the main the wind gusted.

In a rolling sea with the wind now howling, under a dim spreader light, I tied myself to the mast to set a double-reefed main. It was like trying to thread a needle atop a galloping horse. Somehow I managed to get the sail set and crawl back to the cockpit. *Nalani* was loping along at 8.5 knots on the meter, and the autopilot was struggling to stay on course. The swell pushed the stern and the wind pulled the bow; *Nalani* rose and dove and the seas washed over the side decks. I hesitated. We were clearly over-canvassed, but I had no interest in climbing back on deck in those conditions. If I waited the wind might ease, but if it got worse we'd be in trouble.

A half-hour later I decided to act. I clipped on a harness and crawled up the rolling deck to tie myself once again to the mast, thankful for the new pulpits. The sea slapped against the hull and drenched me while the wind howled in my ears. Speech was impossible. I hand-signaled Karin to turn the helm into the wind. *Nalani* slowed as the sails spilled wind; I dropped the main quickly, looping it with a couple of quick ties. We fell back off wind and I scrambled back to the cockpit.

We slowed to six knots and were no longer crashing into the seas. We settled into a rhythm and the autopilot steered without a struggle. Below there was still a chorus of clunks, slaps, ringing, and bangs, but we were under control. We ran under staysail through the rest of the night.

By dawn the wind had blown itself out and the swell had shifted aft. We reverted to power and enjoyed an easier ride, without being tossed side to side. Late morning we fetched Culebra and motored into Ensenada Honda, setting our anchor off Dewey. It had been 25 hours since we left the Lagoon. We had not slept nor eaten anything but granola bars. We sat back in the cockpit and simply luxuriated in the flat calm and quiet of the harbor. After lunch we went below for a long nap.

The next morning we spread out the charts. We measured the distance from Culebra to Rum Cay in the southern Bahamas and discovered it was roughly the same as we had traveled since leaving Trinidad. From Rum Cay we would have to sail to Georgetown, run up the Exuma chain, cross northwest past New Providence to Chubb Cay, and then cross the Banks and the gulf stream to Florida. After that we had to round southern Florida and make our way up the west coast to Tampa. After five months of moving north, we still had a long way to go. We decided to stay at Culebra for a few days to rest up, and to tour San Juan.

In the dark before dawn we ran the dinghy through the canal to the ocean side of Dewey and tied up at the town docks. We boarded the husky, worn commercial ferry to Fajardo, Puerto Rico. It was a pleasant trip over easy seas, taking an hour and a half. At the ferry terminal in Fajardo we found a maxi-taxi headed to Rio Piedras, where we were told we could pick up a bus into San Juan.

We drove over several small mountains through scenic country before we emerged into urban sprawl. The driver picked up a few additional fares along the way, and the roads became crowded with morning traffic. He wove recklessly across lanes, passing stalled traffic by driving on the shoulder.

We were in thick traffic when his cell phone rang. He spoke rapidly and was clearly distracted. Brake lights glowed ahead of us. He regained his wits at the last possible moment and slammed on the brakes, screeching and sliding towards the stopped cars. Luckily a small space opened in the lane next to us. He veered into it, barely avoiding the car ahead of us, and came to a stop inches from another car.

At Rio Piedras, an hour and a half after leaving the ferry docks, our driver offered to take us into San Juan for a mere $60. Since the bus fare was fifty cents each we politely refused. He dropped us at a maxi-taxi stop, claiming that was far as he was allowed to go. We had to walk across town to find the AMA bus terminal.

"Donde' esta el autobus a' Old San Juan?" I asked the bus controller in confident Spanish.

"Si, numero cinq," he responded, offering the lane number. We wandered across the terminal to the bus lanes and found our bus.

We then learned that we needed exact change of four quarters. The driver would not accept a dollar bill. Nobody nearby had change. There were no change machines in the bus terminal. We returned to the controller who shook his head, as if nobody had ever asked for change. Back on the streets, we walked over to a taxi and the driver reluctantly exchanged four quarters for a dollar. We returned to the bus and triumphantly dropped our quarters into the glass fare machine.

The bus ran through downtown San Juan and then across a river past the cruise ship area to Old San Juan. It stopped frequently, picking up and discharging people, on their way somewhere important. Most of the women dressed provocatively (by our standards) in low-cut tops with bare midriffs. There were several stunning young women who seemed out of place on a bus. There were also large women with thick rolls of flesh spilling from tightly wrapped breasts. The men were either thin and circumspect, or chubby and jovial. The extremes were interesting to us, unlike anything we had seen on any other island.

We stepped off the bus four hours after leaving Culebra. With a street map in hand we wandered into Old San Juan, which is a village built on a bluff overlooking the harbor entrance. The streets are narrow and steep, paved with cobblestones of a pleasant blue hue. The buildings are brick and stone with flat roofs, originally built when Puerto Rico was colonized by Spain in the 16th and 17th centuries.

We climbed the hill to visit the town fort and to walk along the ocean road. A steep wall protected the city from the bluffs and on the other side was a sprawling slum. At the heights across from the old fort was a park. There were dozens of people flying kites, all dressed in blue shirts.

The fort is a massive structure of rock built on the corner of town which overlooks the harbor entrance. It looms protectively over the harbor and casts a shadow on the town. It is hard to imagine any unfriendly ship surviving its cannons. There are tunnels and pathways to a network of rooms, some with windows and others enclosed. Black cannons aim out over the harbor.

We returned to town for lunch. There were many bars and restaurants, but they all seemed to cater to tourists. We wanted something more authentic. We finally found a small bar with lunch tables that appeared local. We ordered several tapas, but they were disappointingly mediocre. The sangria was excellent, but outrageously priced at $7.50 a glass. We left disappointed.

We took a bus back to Rio Piedras and crossed town to the maxi-taxi stop. There were no taxis in sight. We waited a few minutes and then asked a street cleaner who directed us to a different bus terminal. There we found a bus to Fajardo. The driver waited a full 45 minutes until every seat was filled. There was apparently no schedule. Along the way he stopped for additional people who stood in the aisles. When the aisles filled up he stopped again and somehow stuffed in another fare.

We arrived in downtown Fajardo a few hours before our return ferry was scheduled to leave. We walked around the town and out to the docks where we had a beer and then walked up a hill through a neighborhood to a small hotel. There we drank another beer and feasted on stuffed potato skins, in air-conditioning.

On the return ferry to Culebra we watched the sun set over the sea. We were tired but happy. Our experience on the mainland had been pleasant. The people were friendly and helpful. We never sensed any danger, even when walking through the poorer neighborhoods.

At the docks we found our dinghy tied up and waiting. We returned through the canal to Ensenada Honda and *Nalani*.

CULEBRA TO SOUTH CAICOS

The morning we motored out of Ensenada Honda was clear, with a light easterly breeze. After rounding the southeast corner of Culebra, we set sail for Cayo de Luis Pena, keeping well off the coast of Culebra. We stayed on a broad reach fifteen degrees south of our course line. Any closer to course and our sails began to flap and we lost speed. *Nalani* was not equipped to run directly downwind. We jibed side to side instead, averaging course, much like tacking upwind.

The steady breeze carried us past Cayo de Luis Pena to Cabo Lobo, where we jibed north keeping to the east of Cabo Lobito. We hardened sails and headed out of the Sonda de Vieques into the Atlantic Ocean. This took us north of the island chain and reefs that string from Culebra to Puerto Rico like a necklace. After giving the islands some space, we were able to ease off and head for the Turks and Caicos.

Our course aimed north of Puerto Rico and the Dominican Republic and was dead downwind. For the next five days we would jibe from one broad reach to another, working our way across 500 miles of ocean.

Late that afternoon the day turned black. To the south, along the coast of Puerto Rico, huge squalls billowed, forming a black curtain that hid the mountains. More squalls formed ahead of us, wrapping into a large arc northward and then east behind us. We were inside a small bowl of blue sky surrounded by black, stormy weather. It was eerily like the eye of a hurricane. The storms sucked the wind away. We dropped sail and crept warily ahead under power.

We had known that a trough would move east through the area that day, and we had discussed waiting for it to pass. However, as good superstitious sailors we did not want to leave on a Friday. We decided instead to sail through the trough, to get to the better weather behind it. At that moment, enveloped by a wall of storms, we doubted the wisdom of our decision.

We motored for six hours. There was not a wisp of wind and the seas were flat. Enormous black clouds flashed bright strokes of lightning all around us. It was a long, fretful, six hours. Night fell, and we ran inside a bowl of black illuminated sporadically by distant lightning. Then, a sprinkle of stars broke out and a slight breeze came up. We had emerged safely on the other side of the trough.

The wind freshened and the sky filled with stars. We shut down the engine and set sail, loping along at a comfortable four knots. We sailed through the night, jibing one long reach to another, staggering northwest towards the Turks and Caicos.

Around noon the next day the wind picked up and our speed increased. The seas built from an easy three foot swell to six feet, and eventually eight and ten foot swells became frequent. During the worst of it a wave broke over the side and drenched Karin.

Nalani sailed well under wind vane control, turning her butt to the swells and rolling side to side. She seemed to enjoy the rollicking, but we were not as comfortable. The wind built to twenty knots. Stores rattled and banged; water in the tanks sloshed back and forth; seas slapped the hull; the decks creaked and moaned; the rigging flapped and rang. We crossed the Mona Passage south of the Mona Canyon.

We settled into a routine, running one broad reach for several hours and then jibing to the other side. We loped along at six knots, averaging maybe four on course. We watched the water slide by and grabbed handholds for every step.

At meal times we heated up a can of food. Preparing a normal meal was out of the question. We stood over the stove, bracing against the roll, tilting the pot to keep it from spilling. We passed bowls to the cockpit and ate while *Nalani* rolled side to side, and her bow lifted and dropped. We drank after eating, since we could not manage a glass and a bowl together. Washing the dishes was a juggling chore. To use the head, we had to wedge ourselves against the cabinets and keep a careful eye on the water level in the bowl.

There were no whales, no dolphins, no jumping fish, no birds, and no land; there was nothing but a rolling sea, whipped to froth in the wind. We could not read. It was too noisy to sleep below. Instead, we took short naps on the downwind cockpit seat. We plotted X's on a rocking chart, ticking off the miles.

We ran like this north of the Dominican Republic and south of the Navidad Banks to the southern edge of the Silver Banks. We kept a wary eye on our position, jibing away from the shallow water on the Banks as the current and the wind pushed us towards them. To run up on the Banks in these conditions would be disastrous. We crossed the Silver Banks passage and ran south of the Mouchoir Banks, rolling and rocking, jibe after jibe. We ate and slept in spurts, and in between we stared at the endless rolling sea.

On the fourth night we crossed the Mouchoir Passage and headed for Great Sand Cay, a small island south of Grand Turk. It had a cove off a sandy beach with a straightforward approach, and we were somewhat familiar with it, having stopped there on our way south. We could have sailed by to reach South Caicos the next morning, but the lure of an anchorage and some uninterrupted sleep was too tempting.

There was a good moon and the beach glowed in a welcoming arc. We nuzzled up into fifteen feet of water and dropped our anchor near midnight. It hooked easily in the good sand bottom. Although we rocked a little in the surge, the overall calm in the island's lee was euphoric. It was quiet but for a chorus of squawking birds. We shared a glass of wine and then slept like rocks, in our bed for the first time in four days.

We awoke by alarm early to get an update on the weather. Those few hours of sleep were the best sleep we have ever enjoyed. We were right to have stopped instead of continuing on through the night. After breakfast we headed to sea again, across the Turks channel to South Caicos. The seas were easy and the motion was comfortable. It was a clear and beautiful day and we were revitalized by the rest. Never underestimate the value of sleep. We enjoyed a fine sail to end an arduous journey.

We made Cockburn Harbor early that afternoon, five days after leaving Culebra. After clearing customs and tidying up *Nalani*, we shared a couple of cold beers in the cockpit, gazing fondly around the calm harbor.

COCKBURN HARBOR
SOUTH CAICOS
21° 29' N 71° 32' W

Our first morning in Cockburn Harbor we woke to rain, which continued all day. After allowing time for a good rinse, we opened the deck fills to let the rain flow down the side decks and into our fresh water tanks. Below, we rested and read. A Low had formed over the southeast Bahamas and bad weather was forecast for the next several days. We were happy to be tucked in, well up Cockburn Harbor, to wait it out.

The next day was cloudy with periods of light rain. We took the dinghy into town and walked to the house that served as the local internet cafe. We checked our emails and introduced ourselves to a woman filling out a pile of forms for the port manager. She was Christine, owner and captain of *Gypsy Spirit*, a Watkins 36 sloop.

Christine had single-handed from West Palm Beach, Florida, buddy-boating with her friend Ed who also single-handed. They had left Mayaguana together, taking the ocean route north of the Turks and Caicos. They lost each other in the frequent squalls and heavy seas. Christine decided to seek refuge at South Caicos. However, she had no charts; her laptop with its electronic charts had broken in one of the storms. She had no paper backups.

The seas were rough as night descended. There were constant squalls with heavy rain and no visibility. She lost her engine when an air bubble formed in the fuel line from the rocking and tossing seas. She disabled her autopilot to save its battery and hove-to, to await dawn.

That night she spotted a ship heading towards her. She thought it would pass to starboard by the look of its bow lights. The ship was the 268 foot cargo ship, *Tropic Opal*. She was returning empty from her regular weekly run between Florida and the Turks and Caicos. As she passed by *Gypsy Spirit* she side-swiped the sloop. The captain had spotted a momentary blip on his radar, but he had assumed it was sea clutter, common in stormy weather. He saw no navigation lights. He didn't even know he had hit the other boat.

Christine was huddled below trying to keep dry. She heard a horrible crunch and scraping sound and looked up to see a cliff looming skyward. She was terrified but kept her wits and hailed the ship on the VHF. The captain turned his ship around and came to her assistance. She transferred to his ship and they towed the broken sloop to port.

Christine related this story as she filled out forms. Afterwards, we took her to lunch. She was a strong person, but clearly rattled. We suggested that before any repairs were made she should take a complete set of pictures. Her camera was broken too, so we walked back to the pier with her and took a set of pictures with our camera.

The rigging was torn and the mast was separated at the spreaders, its top half strapped on deck. The sails were ripped and fluttered in the breeze. The hull was badly scraped. The forward bulkhead tabbing had separated from the hull and the hull-to-deck joint was ripped open in several places. Below was a shambles. Water seeped inside, tripping the bilge pump in regular spurts.

Late that night her friend Ed arrived and anchored. We hailed him the next morning and told him about our day with Christine. He already knew of her trouble, having heard from another boater.

We were glad we had left Culebra that one day early, to reach Cockburn Harbor before the bad weather hit. There were three days and nights of squalls, rain, and gusting winds. It was not weather to be out and about, if you had a choice.

The next weekend we crossed the Banks to Provo under blue skies on a brisk beam reach. There was only a light wind chop, and we sat on deck enjoying the ride while the autopilot steered from waypoint to waypoint. Our job was to scan the light blue water for black coral heads. We had to relieve the autopilot seven or eight times, when our course would have taken us over a head. Approaching Sapodilla Bay the wind strengthened. It was an exhilarating race to the finish after a fine day's sail. We arrived two hours ahead of our planned schedule.

That night we watched the glow worms come out, admiring the inventiveness of nature. The female floats on the surface spinning in an ever-widening spiral, releasing a trail of luminescent eggs. The spiral spreads slowly and merges into a plate of green glow. Soon you spot a blinking torpedo a few feet away steaming full speed at the plate. They collide in an explosion of light as the male fertilizes the eggs. Then the phosphorescence dissolves. The show continued for about ten minutes.

The next day was Easter Sunday, and after a traditional breakfast of hard-boiled eggs and sausage we sailed the dinghy around the bay and walked the beach. That night we celebrated with rum and tonics, followed by a canned ham, baked with yams in a honey-mustard sauce. We served it with baked beans and a bottle of Chardonnay. After dinner we were again entertained by worm sex.

Unicorn arrived the next day and invited us for dinner. We rowed over for a delicious meal of cabbage and potatoes prepared by Olena, followed by an outstanding chocolate desert made from Grenada chocolate factory bars. There was plenty of wine and good conversation.

Satiated and happy, we slowly drifted our dinghy back to *Nalani* on glassy water under a black sky, flush with bright white stars.

ABRAHAMS BAY
MAYAGUANA
22° 22' N 73° 00' W

We left Provo on a calm, sunny day, and ran along the Sandbore channel to the western edge of the Banks. There, we turned north and followed a natural channel we had noticed on the charts. It wound through shallows and reefs to a pool of clear water with a sand bottom. We wanted to stage there to get an early start the next day.

The pool was ten feet deep and about a hundred yards wide. The water was crystal clear and calm. We could see shells on the bottom, lying on white sand, and fish swimming below us. As we gazed west we could see the blue channel snaking from our hole through creamy-white shallows into the dark blue of deep water.

The water was so clear we appeared suspended in air. There was no land in sight, only rippled blue water in every direction out to a circle of horizon. We floated alone, a tiny spec on a great sea, tethered by our small anchor. It was exhilarating, but it was also nerve wracking, to be so alone and vulnerable.

We swam and snorkeled around *Nalani* in our private pool, as clear and calm as any home pool. The only differences were the occasional small fish that swam by, sand dollars lying on the bottom, and the black anchor chain arcing from our home to a partially buried anchor.

We watched the sun set that night, feeling our significance dwindle, afloat on a vast sea under a sky billowing in vibrant reds, yellows, and oranges.

The next morning we retraced our path through the reefs back to the Sandbore channel, and then off the Banks. We motored all day over flat seas across the Caicos Passage to Mayaguana, running along the southern shore and turning into Abraham's Bay at its wider and deeper western entrance. We motored back east across the bay, keeping a good lookout for the numerous coral heads. They were easy to spot in good visibility, but would be impossible on a cloudy day. Even infrequent shadows from small white clouds made it difficult to determine the water depth. As we navigated the eastern half of the bay the water became more shallow, and we gave up a good mile and a half from the settlement.

The next morning we took the dinghy to the settlement of Abraham's Bay. The water was shallow and clear, but whipped up by a steady fifteen knot breeze. We tacked the engine upwind, to avoid crashing directly into the chop, but we were still splashed frequently. We kept a sharp lookout for coral heads which hid inches below the surface. It was a long and wet mile and a half.

At the top of the bay we found the marked channel to the town jetty. It was narrow and shallow, less than two feet deep in places and maybe four feet wide. We beached the dinghy inside the jetty, tying her to a discarded wooden cable spool.

Mayaguana is a sparsely populated island; there are only a few hundred residents distributed across three settlements. The bulk of the island is thickly wooded. Since it is the southernmost island of the Bahamas, it has a customs outpost.

It was a short hike from the jetty to the government complex at the edge of the settlement. The complex was a group of small shacks that housed customs, the telephone company, and the port authority. The woman behind the counter greeted us warmly and then apologized that she did not have the authority to clear us. The Customs officer, who was also the local police, was at the airport. She would call him, but it might be some time before he could make it back. We were free to walk around and explore in the meantime.

The dirt road from the government complex led into the village, which was only a few roads, sprinkled with small houses. They were clean and well kept, but austere. The road then exited the village and led to the other settlements. There were two small restaurants in town, both closed. We walked every street in less than an hour.

When we returned to Customs, the officer was still absent. We asked about lunch, and the clerk phoned Ned, who cooked meals to order in his home kitchen. She ordered three lunches, for us and herself, and then called the Customs/Police officer. She handed me the phone.

"I have to inspect your boat," he said.

"Fine, but it's an hour ride by dinghy and the wind is blowing pretty good."

"Oh no mon, I am from Nassau. I got no sea legs. Just move the boat around to Low Point. You can anchor near the dock. Do you know where it is?"

"We can't cross the bay," I answered. "It's too windy and the visibility is bad. We have a six foot draft."

"Well, maybe tomorrow?"

"Maybe," I stalled. "But the weather is supposed to get worse."

"Yah mon, maybe tomorrow." He hung up.

Our friendly clerk, having overheard the conversation, then made another call. In a few minutes a different customs officer arrived. Apparently, they had more than one after all. We explained our story and she called the boss back. After a lively discussion, he decided to let her take our $300 and be done with it. She made us state that we had no firearms and nothing illegal aboard. We were then officially cleared into the Bahamas.

The business over we called Ned back to add another lunch. We offered to pick up the lunches and found his home easily, having passed by it on our earlier walk. We knocked at the front door and Ned handed us several bags.

We returned to Customs and were ushered into an office. The women set out lunch on a desk. It was chicken braised in an onion sauce, with rice, potato salad, and a pasta salad. We shared the food while carrying on a friendly and relaxed conversation. They were curious about us and where we had cruised, and we questioned them on the history and current state of Mayaguana.

FISHERMAN'S BAY
SAMANA
23° 04' N 73° 45' W

Samana is a small, uninhabited island in the southern Bahamas. It is rarely visited by cruisers, in part due its remote location, about 20 miles northeast of Acklins Island off the normal cruising path. Samana also has a difficult and unmarked channel into Fisherman's Bay, its sole protected waters. The channel weaves a thin, dangerous path through the fringing coral reef. Once inside the reef, anchored boats are protected from high waves and storms, but it is not comfortable. There is a constant roll, which changes direction on the tide and wind.

For the adventuresome few that make their way there, Samana is a gem. The shoreline is a lovely contrast of white cliffs, scrub brush, rock formations, and flat sand. The waters are clear and packed with live reefs full of colorful fish. It is untrammeled by human existence, except for a few wooden fishing huts and remnants of old stone buildings. The huts occasionally serve as temporary homes to fishermen from Acklins Island who collect cascarilla bark, black land crabs, conch, lobster, and fish.

Samana is about ten miles long and two miles wide and the interior is hills of scrub brush and rock. The National Geographic Society published a study claiming Samana was the first landfall of Columbus in the new world. While this has not been universally accepted, it has not been refuted either and remains a good possibility. At the time of Columbus, the island was home to Lucayan Indians.

Samana pulled us like a magnet. We felt seasoned enough to handle the channel, and we looked forward to the feel of a deserted island before our final run homeward.

From Abraham's Bay we sailed west around Devil's Point and up the west coast of Mayaguana. We anchored off Northwest point, in time for a fierce squall. Our anchor held, but we spent a nervous night on the narrow shelf between ocean depths and rocky shore. We were underway early the next morning and sailed downwind on six foot rolling seas to Samana. We made the published waypoint outside the channel a few hours before sunset.

We dropped our sails and slowly motored towards the island, following the recommended course. We nervously studied the water and monitored the depth gauge. We were heading directly at the black fringing reef, but we saw no channel. We could only run the course and stay alert.

We saw what looked like a channel and steered into it. There was no sandy bottom to follow and there was no room to turn around. We had to keep going and trust we had found the right channel. We followed the color changes, the only way to keep to the deeper water. The channel was crooked and narrow and there were dangerous coral heads on either side. We trusted our eyes and steered. If we missed a turn there was nobody to help.

There were a couple of small floats that marked something, but we couldn't trust them to be in the right position. We left them to starboard and emerged into deeper water with a sandy bottom. We turned behind Propeller Cay and anchored.

After stowing sails we poured rum and tonics, heavy on the rum.

We were alone. There were no other boats at Samana. We had the entire 18 square miles of land, and the bays and reefs to ourselves. It was an eerie but wonderful feeling. We were eager to explore.

The first morning we enjoyed a breakfast of eggs and sausage, with large chunks of cheese, bean dip, and bread. After cleaning up, we slathered on sunscreen, gathered our snorkel gear, and climbed into the dinghy. We ran east, past the channel to the white cliffs along the coast. The bottom was all coral reefs, some close to the surface. We moved slowly, studying the colors and weaving among the stands. We found a break and turned into the beach.

We walked maybe a half-mile down the beach. The sand gave way to rocky shelves, low cliffs, and large standing rocks. The beach itself was eroded from the land, forming a steep hill a few feet inland. We climbed the hill in several places to view fields of scrub brush and rocks and higher hills inland. It was inhospitable but beautiful, a dry and hardy land.

We collected shells and stepped over the remnants of humanity that floated in with the tide. There were plastic buckets and baskets, fish floats and lines, and one perfectly intact light bulb. The view out to sea was spectacular. The creamy white and light blue shallows were framed by black reefs, which yielded to the white froth of breaking waves. Beyond the reef a lavender sea stretched to the horizon where it dissolved into a soft blue sky. Puffy white clouds drifted overhead. We stopped several times to simply admire the view.

We ran the dinghy back through the reefs to Fisherman's Bay, continuing up the shallow bay to its northern end. There we found shacks in various states of disrepair. One had an old generator at its side, which looked like it might still run. Several had blankets or other remnants of the fisherman who last used them. We climbed the hill behind the shacks to find only a larger hill inland. To the right of the shacks was a dry tidal flat.

As we explored the tide ran out. We had to walk the dinghy out a hundred yards before we found enough depth to dip the engine. Once in deeper water we spotted a coral head and flopped overboard with face mask and fins. There were blue tangs, yellow-tail snappers, red snappers, silver fish, and schools of rainbow fish, striped in blue, red and yellow. We saw what looked like a lion fish. There were branching corals, brain coral, and sea fans.

We then took the dinghy to explore the wide beach near the Columbus Anchorage. The water was rough with a wind driven two-foot chop and we had a rousing run through a cut in the reefs to the beach. It was a flat and wide beach and not too interesting. We ran back out the gap in the reefs and returned to *Nalani*. That night we enjoyed cocktails and dinner under a black starry sky.

We awoke refreshed the next day. After a blueberry pancake breakfast we launched the dinghy for more exploration. We found a path through the reefs to the beach immediately across from *Nalani*. There, we found a grave, its headstone announcing "born 1906 and died 1966." The name was too washed out to read, and the brush too thick to get close.

We discovered a green bottle in the sand with a metal screw cap and a note inside. The language is maybe Portuguese, but we are not certain. Since the author undoubtedly wanted the note to be read, we repeat the legible phrases:

4-06-2003
De Beuno Jose Dantes de Campos
ti:
Um dia calmo sem chuva, sem ren …
me de o rarinho que um diem ja tive …
,que me geomfanhaste sempque …
Amor e carirshe derite vide …

mas rom grande falta de algruem
… temjestade como ma bomanca, que
… coracai e troureste luz aos' meus
… fra so' jur breves instantes
… naudade que me acomfanha no
Lia do meu roracao
… ensagem diz alguma Poisa a minha
4950 Moncad-Portugal

Our apologies to the author for the spellings and omissions; the note was difficult to read. We took photographs, resealed the bottle, and left it in place.

We then ran across the water to Propeller Cay, to snorkel the reefs along its edge. We marveled at the clarity of the water and the beautiful fish of all colors. The reef stretched for hundreds of yards and the snorkeling was some of the most spectacular we've experienced.

Our anchorage became more rolly each day. A cold front was making its way south. It was impossible to find a calm place because the direction of the roll changed during the day. It had to do with the winds, cross-currents, and tides. It was not comfortable, which encouraged us to continue our explorations. We returned to the fishermans' huts and walked to the tidal flats. There were pools of water leftover from high tide. Among the mangrove roots were thousands of small, black conch, maybe a ¼ inch long. It was a nursery.

We began to worry about our water supply. With a cold front coming and gales to the north the seas were expected to build to twelve feet in the northern Bahamas. We might have to stay another week, and our fresh water was dwindling. We bathed in the sea and rinsed in fresh water to conserve, and at night we set up to catch rain. It blew hard for a couple days and we stayed aboard and read. We were protected by the island from north and easterly winds, so it was not too bad. Outside the reef was another question. We could see high swells and whipped up waves. We were happy in our protected harbor, but we continued to worry about our water supply.

On Saturday, our sixth day at Samana, Karin kneaded pizza dough. After it rose she rolled it out and we spread on tomato pesto, sautéed onions and garlic, chopped chayote, and canned chicken. We folded and baked it until brown for a delicious lunch. Afterwards, we stepped on deck to discover a yawl had anchored inside Fisherman's bay. We had been so busy with the dough we had not noticed their arrival. What was somebody else doing at our island? The winds were too strong to venture out to meet them.

Sunday was calm but overcast and cold, a bone-chilling 70°F (probably 68° with the wind chill). We ventured out to collect shells and stopped at the yawl *Seminole* to introduce ourselves. We were invited to dinner and cocktails the next day, which we happily accepted.

For our social encounter, we arrived late afternoon with a bottle of wine and some bean dip. Elizabeth and Michael welcomed us aboard and set out cheese, eggplant salad, and assorted appetizers on deck. They opened a delicious bottle of champagne. We learned that *Seminole* was built in 1916. All 47 feet of the wood yacht had been meticulously restored in Maine. The decks, masts, and trim, including blocks and tackles, were all freshly hewn from clear grained wood and immaculately varnished. We admired the boat, sipped Champagne, and enjoyed the snacks, in the beautiful setting of Fisherman's bay.

Below were modern electronics, a water maker, and some appliances. Otherwise, the interior was traditional. We enjoyed a chicken-rice stew served, incredibly, with a fresh salad. Greens are unheard of at sea. Our hosts opened several bottles of red wine, and we exchanged stories. We learned that they do not live aboard, but rather fly back and forth from Maine for a few weeks at a time to cruise. That explained the salad. They generously offered us fresh water, supplies, and the use of their satellite phone – whatever we needed. We thanked them, but admitted to needing nothing at the moment. Everyone got a bit tipsy and we had a grand time.

Back on *Nalani* we cut our water use again, to around two gallons a day, and waited for good weather to leave.

CLARENCE TOWN
LONG ISLAND
23° 06' N 74° 57' W

We left Fisherman's Bay at noon, to ensure good light to navigate the channel. We used the small buoys to orient ourselves, and found the water easier to read than on our way inside. Once clear of the reef, we turned west and followed its outline into the Columbus anchorage. We had decided to stay there overnight for a dawn departure the next day. We wanted a full day to reach Crooked Island.

The Columbus anchorage is really open ocean, protected to the north by Samana and to the east by the reef that encloses Fisherman's Bay. It is never calm, but in the right conditions it is safe. We found a spot close to the beach, but we still spent an uncomfortable night exposed to swell. We were up before dawn the next morning, anxious to leave.

We ran all day towards Crooked Island with a poled-out jib and a low rpm engine, dragging a colorful lure in hopes of catching a fish. The gale driven swell had peaked, and it softened more each hour. Still, we rocked and rolled our way southwest on a slight breeze. After noon we spotted Bird Rock, off the tip of Crooked Island. I climbed on deck to drop the jib to prepare to jibe. Suddenly the fishing pole bent and its reel whizzed. I ran back to the cockpit while Karin cut us into the wind to drift.

I reeled in the heavy fish, spotting a flash of iridescent yellow near the surface. At that moment the fish ran; the drag exploded and line flew off the reel. I watched the line run out, hoping there was enough. When the drag silenced I resumed reeling. About twenty feet from *Nalani* the fish exploded out of the water and twisted skyward. It was a beautiful dorado (dolphin fish, also known as mahi-mahi). The beauty and size of the fish was incredible. I kept reeling and he jumped twice more, trying to shake the hook off. I pulled him up to the hull and handed the pole to Karin.

As I leaned over with a gaff hook I was surprised to see three other dorado circling the caught fish. One lunged at him. This shocked us both until we saw that the artificial squid had run up the line away from the hook. The other fish had gone after it. I hooked our fish in the gills and hauled him up on the side deck. I had landed my first dorado.

Karin brought out a bottle of rum and dumped a shot into his gills. He flopped excitedly and threw off copious amounts of blood and scales. It took three more shots to finish him, during which he regurgitated a whole flying fish.

Our conflicted emotions intensified as the iridescence of his bright colors dimmed. We were sad to have killed such a beautiful creature, but we were not so sad as to forego the delicious meat. I worked fast to avoid thinking about it. I stabbed into his backbone behind his head to ensure he was dead. I then filleted him on deck and dropped the carcass overboard, to feed other sea creatures. We spent the next twenty minutes swabbing the deck of blood, scales, and slime.

Our dorado measured 34 inches from the head to the base of the tail. The head was seven inches across. He was a good size, but not huge. We bagged three large dinners of all white meat. I had been rather sloppy with the cutting and we probably could have had another meal, but it was enough for us. The rest of the meat would not go to waste in the sea.

We motored past Pittstown Point and anchored on the narrow shelf between land and the depths. It was a beautiful sand bottom off a pretty beach sparsely populated with houses. I sprinkled our first dorado portion with Cajun spices and flour and fried it for dinner. It was incredibly delicious.

The next morning we motored north a few hours before a breeze came up and we could sail. It was then a close reach over easing seas under sunny skies. Arriving off Clarence Town we hailed the Flying Fish Marina.

We asked for a slip for a few days to fill up on water and diesel, do laundry, and stock up on groceries. We were politely refused; they would only accept power boats. At this time of year, large sport fish boats prowl the seas around Long and Cat islands. The marina keeps its slips open for these diesel hungry boats. It's hard to blame them. The money we would spend would be a pittance compared to a sport fish boat.

We motored into the harbor past the marina and turned up into the anchorage. The water was calm and clear, a light blue over grassy sand. We found a patch of good sand for our anchor among the grass. The harbor was immense, but outside of the anchorage it was very shallow. Low lying white cays surrounded and protected the waters.

We launched the dinghy and doubled back to the marina. We scouted the fuel dock and found an easy access with enough depth for *Nalani*. They had a laundry room and a bar/restaurant overlooking the harbor. It was small and simple, but well kept and clean. We asked about internet service and were told that the marina does not share its connection. There was service in town.

We walked up the road to the Shell station which advertised internet. There was one PC set up in a corner with dial-up access. We tried several times to get into our email without success. We gave up and telephoned family instead.

We returned to *Nalani* to gather up our dirty laundry and ran back to the marina. We spent the late afternoon and early evening feeding money into washers and dryers. Between loads we hung out in the restaurant, having a few beers and a dinner of fried conch and fish sandwich. It was 9 p.m. when we finally returned to *Nalani*, satiated and tired with clean clothes.

The next day we walked around the settlement of Clarence Town, taking pictures of Father Jerome's churches. The town was sparsely populated, tidy, and clean. The people were friendly. A car stopped to ask us if we needed a ride anywhere, or any other assistance. We enjoyed conch gumbo and fried grouper for lunch at the Harbor restaurant.

We stayed three days, exploring the bay waters inside Salt Pond Cay and Clem Cay, and the cuts out to sea. The water was crystal clear over white sand and grass; the beaches were white, and backed by reef cliffs and scrub flat lands. The bay was shallow, too shallow even for our dinghy at low tide. There was one deep blue hole near Clem Cay with depths of 40 feet.

We surveyed the waters and enjoyed walking the beaches. We followed turtles, a foot wide, and a number of rays, one of which was three feet wide. We saw barracuda and a small shark. Karin collected a few sea biscuits. Between our field trips, we ran into town for supplies and took *Nalani* to the marina to top up our diesel and fresh water.

From Clarence Town we sailed to Rum Cay, and anchored off Port Nelson. It was very rolly and uncomfortable. The settlement consisted of five north/south streets intersected with three east/west streets. There were two restaurants, a few stores, and a Batelco office. The few houses were spaced out with empty lots between them. The people we met were happy and friendly, but there just wasn't much there. We drank a couple of beers in a restaurant with a sand floor and left the next day for Conception Island.

CONCEPTION ISLAND
BAHAMAS
23° 51' N 75° 08' W

We motored into West Bay, Conception Island, one of our favorite places. The water was vividly clear over a bottom of soft white sand, framed by a long arc of beautiful beach. It was early afternoon and the sky was bright blue. We were surprised to find seven sailboats, two mega-yachts, a small motor yacht, and a large sport fish. We had never seen it so crowded, but the anchorage was large and the boats were well spread out.

Conception Island is an uninhabited nature reserve, a short day sail east of Georgetown where the Exuma Sound meets the Atlantic Ocean. It is northwest of Rum Cay and west of San Salvador. There are two anchorages: West Bay and East Bay. In all but a westerly blow, West Bay is preferred. East Bay has a trickier entrance through reefs and is exposed to the Atlantic Ocean. West Bay has a wide and easy entrance and is usually wonderfully calm.

The island has gorgeous beaches on both sides and interior salt ponds and creeks that provide a sea life hatchery. It is renowned for bonefish, and is home to juveniles of many species of fish and birds, including turtles and sharks. Off its eastern Atlantic shore there are miles of black coral reefs, beautiful when observed from land, but dangerous at sea.

We stayed three days, walking the beach, swimming, and taking dinghy excursions. It was a vacation of sorts, time off from the work of cruising. We snorkeled the massive coral heads off the eastern shore. There were brain coral, stag horn, pillar, and others. We observed the usual suspects, blue tangs, parrot fish, and the like. Much of the coral rose to within a few inches of the surface forcing us to run the dinghy like a downhill slalom. We stopped at East Bay and walked along its magnificent white-pink sand beach, gazing out at the blue ocean and black reefs.

Two mornings we ran our dinghy into the inland lake on fast incoming tides. The rushing blue water wrapped around the entrance shoal, cutting a turbulent path through the white sand. We explored the pond and its channels, marveling at the abundant wildlife. We cruised by turtles and through schools of fish in the shallows. There were many varieties of sea birds. In a deep hole we watched a shark swim in circles.

THE RUN HOME

We left Conception Island determined to return to Florida without delay. We had reached the point in time when you know you are done and you are ready to go home. We sailed on good winds to Hawks Nest Point, Cat Island, and the next day across Exuma Sound to Dotham Cut, where we anchored off Black Point. The wind then deserted us. We motored north along the Exuma islands staying overnight at Shroud and Highborne Cays. We then crossed the Yellow Banks to Rose Island near Nassau.

We continued the next day over calm seas to the Berry Islands. We planned to spend a few days at Frazier's Hog Cay Marina to top up our water and fuel and relax before crossing the Banks. As we approached Chubb Cay we hailed the marina several times. Silence. We then hailed Chubb Cay Marina. More silence. We later learned that Frazier's Hog Cay Marina had gone out of business and that Chubb Cay Marina had closed for renovations.

We anchored off the east coast of Chubb Cay, tucking up near the flats. A front came through, and then another, bringing lines of squalls. We waited two days while black storms whipped up the seas with loud cracks of thunder, bright streaks of lightning, and downpours. At least we were able to top up our water tanks. Finally, a brief lull was forecast.

We ran up the Tongue of the Ocean through the Northwest Channel and anchored off Russell Light. The Banks were calm. We floated on twenty feet of clear water with no land in sight. Sea stretched to the horizon in all directions. Overhead wild sculpted clouds, all gray and black, swirled in the blue sky. In the distance they formed into towering thunderheads touching the sea.

It was eerily calm, a contrast that made the churning storms more ominous. On the Banks with land nowhere in sight we were a fragile piece of flotsam, easy prey to the forces of nature. It was awe-inspiring. It struck a chord somewhere deep. We are, after all, animals of nature when you strip away the protections and conveniences of civilization.

The next day we crossed the Banks and emerged into the Gulf Stream at South Riding Rocks. We set the autopilot for Florida. The sun went low into an arc of gray clouds. Streaks of white-yellow sunlight broke through the gray. The sky became a canvas of oranges and reds dabbed with yellows and pools of blue.

Behind us an enormous rainbow formed. It covered half the sky in wide bands of color, creating an arc over the Bahamas. It was a symbolic goodbye, and a thank you, to mark the end to our journey.

EPILOGUE

Two weeks after leaving Conception Island we docked at Marathon Marina in the Florida keys, and cleared back into the U.S. over the phone. After taking on fuel, supplies, and water, we motored two days and one night up the coast to Charlotte Harbor. There were huge squalls all around us, black and threatening, lighting up the night with flashes of white. Somehow, we managed to thread our way between storms.

We crossed Charlotte Harbor and took a slip at Burnt Store Marina. Our cruise, which had begun November 10, 2004 at 13:16, ended when we shut down the engine May 31, 2006 at 15:09.

We stayed with Karin's mom, transitioning into life ashore, and helping her adjust to the loss of Karin's father. We sold *Nalani*, found jobs, and moved to Tampa. We had lived aboard fifteen years. We had cruised to the Bahamas twice, and had now completed a year and a half cruise to Trinidad. We were done.

As cruisers say, we "swallowed the hook" and became land lubbers.

www.ingramcontent.com/pod-product-compliance
Lightning Source LLC
Chambersburg PA
CBHW071453040426
42444CB00008B/1314